P9-DXQ-787

Oven and Rotisserie
ROASTING

David DiResta and Joanne Foran

BRISTOL PUBLISHING ENTERPRISES
San Leandro, California

a nitty gritty® cookbook

©1997 Bristol Publishing Enterprises, Inc., P.O. Box 1737, San Leandro, California 94577. World rights reserved. No part of this publication may be reproduced in any form, nor may it be stored in a retrieval system, transmitted, or otherwise copied for public or private use without prior written permission from the publisher.

Printed in the United States of America.

ISBN 1-55867-167-6

Cover design: Frank J. Paredes
Cover photography: John A. Benson
Food stylist: Susan Massey
Illustrator: James Balkovek

CONTENTS

ABOUT ROASTING

For simple, healthy and delicious cooking, you just can't beat roasting, whether it's with a conventional oven, a portable electric roaster oven or rotisserie. From a main course of tender roasted chicken with a wild rice stuffing, to a grand finale of roasted peaches with shredded coconut, you'll be amazed at the variety and mouth-watering results so easily achieved from this versatile and efficient cooking technique.

Roasting is the oldest and simplest method for food preparation. In roasting, foods are cooked by dry heat, which circulates around the food. For most home cooks, this technique is usually done in a conventional oven. However, roasting can also be done on a spit over a heat source (see *Rotisserie Roasting*, page 139) or in a portable electric roaster oven. Some items, such as chestnuts, can be roasted in a dry skillet, which lends an appetizing, smoky flavor.

Along with old-time favorites, such as roasted turkey and rack of lamb, many unexpected foods can also be roasted. Onions, garlic, potatoes, vegetables and many fruits are delicious and full of flavor when roasted. Another benefit of roasting is that it's easy. Roasting needs very little preparation, usually requires only one pan, produces fabulous results and needs little cleanup. Roasting is an unpretentious honest cooking method for creating comforting meals. It's the perfect vehicle for entertaining because you don't have to monitor the cooking process and you're free to share good times with friends and family members.

ROASTING EQUIPMENT

Here are a few basic items, in addition to an oven, to perfect your roasting talents.

OVEN THERMOMETER

Unfortunately, most factory-installed oven thermometers are grossly inaccurate. Furthermore, the temperature can vary greatly within the confines of the oven's walls. To determine the true temperature in your oven, we strongly recommend purchasing a mercury oven thermometer with a long term warranty from a reputable manufacturer.

PASTRY BRUSH

Pastry brushes are ideally suited for spreading an even coat of liquid or fat on foods without splashing. Choose a pastry brush with natural bristles that are secured firmly to the handle. They can be found at most specialty and cookware shops.

KITCHEN STRING

Kitchen string is an essential tool for trussing poultry and tying roasts, which ensures well-shaped, evenly cooked foods. Look for cotton-based string in a housewares or hardware store, or in the supermarket.

To truss poultry, chop off the wing tips if desired. Position the bird on its back and tuck the wing ends under the neck area. Center a very long piece of kitchen string under the tail portion of the bird, cross the string ends over the tail portion, wind them 1 or 2 times around each leg and pull the legs together securely. Tie a knot securely against the legs. Thread the string ends underneath the wings, close to the body, flip the bird over and tie a knot snugly across the bird's back.

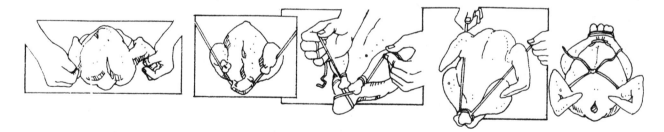

BULB BASTER

Made of heavy-duty plastic, heatproof glass or stainless steel, a bulb baster sucks up pan juices quickly and is perfect for basting roasting foods thoroughly and easily.

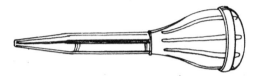

INSTANT-READ MEAT THERMOMETER

An instant-read thermometer is an indispensable cooking tool for acquiring accurate temperature readings in seconds. Purchase a top-quality thermometer to be sure that it will last.

FAT SEPARATOR

Made from heatproof and microwave-safe glass or plastic, this ingenious kitchen device helps remove the fat from gravies and pan drippings. As the fat rises to the top, the remaining juices are poured from the bottom through the spout.

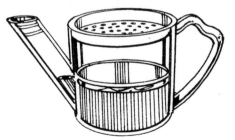

ROASTING RACKS

The best roasting racks are oval, or V-shaped and adjustable, and sit inside the roasting pan to hold meats. Using a rack allows for greater air circulation and helps the fat drain away from the food. For easy cleanup, pick one with a nonstick surface.

ROASTING PANS

To promote the circulation of hot air around the foods you are roasting, use a heavy-gauge, shallow metal roasting pan. The low sides will allow air to flow freely around the food so that it will cook quickly and evenly. The exterior of properly roasted foods should be beautifully browned and the interior thoroughly cooked and moist. To prevent overcrowding the food, it's a good idea to have a variety of sizes of roasting pans. A heavy-gauge pan will also allow you to set it on the stovetop to reduce sauces and pan gravies. When purchasing a roasting pan, look for stainless steel, anodized aluminum, or copper lined with nickel or stainless steel.

PORTABLE ELECTRIC ROASTER OVENS

Portable ovens range in size from 4 to 18 quarts. This unique kitchen appliance is efficient, versatile and convenient, and offers all the benefits of a second oven. Foods cook in this appliance evenly and quickly. The ovens we tested are simple to operate, easy to clean, and heat up quickly without heating up the entire kitchen. All of the recipes in this book will work in a portable electric roaster oven, assuming it is large enough to accommodate the ingredients. Some foods cooked in portable electric roaster ovens require  slightly shorter cooking times than in conventional ovens, but it's best to use an instant-read thermometer for accuracy. Be sure to follow the manufacturer's instructions when using these ovens.

PORTABLE ELECTRIC ROTISSERIES

Roasting foods with these appliances produces moist, flavorful results with no basting and little cleanup. For more on rotisserie roasting, see page 139.

ROASTED ACCOMPANIMENTS

ROASTED PEPPERS

Not only is roasting your own peppers economical, but the flavor is far superior to the bottled variety found in supermarkets. They're wonderful as a side dish for 4 to 6 people along with roasted meats, poultry or fish. Or, chop them finely for a brilliant, smoky addition to sauces, soups, pizza toppings and pasta dishes. To simplify the method and eliminate the arduous task of cleaning the roasted peppers, we strongly recommend that you cut the peppers in half and remove the seeds before roasting. You can use the same technique with other kinds of sweet and spicy peppers.

4 large red, green or yellow bell peppers (about 2 lb.)
1/2 cup olive oil
salt and pepper to taste

Heat grill or broiler to high. Halve peppers lengthwise and remove stems, seeds and membranes. Rinse under cold running water and pat dry. On a work surface, flatten peppers with the heel of your hand and place skin-side down on the grate of grill, or skin-side up under broiler. Roast for 10 to 12 minutes, until skins are charred and blistered. Place charred peppers in a brown paper bag, seal securely and place bag on a plate to prevent leaks. Let peppers sit for at least 20 minutes, until cool enough to handle.

Remove peppers from bag. With your fingers, pull off charred skins and discard. Slice peppers into 1½-inch strips and combine with olive oil, salt and pepper. Refrigerate for at least 2 hours. Serve chilled.

VARIATION: MARINATED ROASTED PEPPERS

Marinate roasted pepper strips in ½ cup olive oil, 1 tbs. white wine vinegar, 1 tsp. dried basil (or 1 tbs. chopped fresh), 1 crushed garlic clove and salt and pepper to taste. Cover and refrigerate for at least 6 hours and up to 1 day, stirring occasionally.

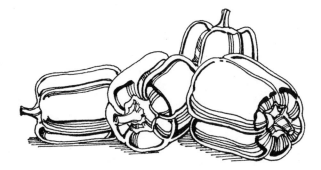

ROASTED CHESTNUTS

Yield: varies

Roasted chestnuts have a distinctive, mild, buttery flavor and greyish-brown nut meat. They're also low in fat and high in fiber. European chestnuts are harvested in the fall of each year and start showing up in stores during October. They're available at most supermarkets, but you'll find the plumpest and freshest variety in Italian specialty markets. Refrigerate unshelled chestnuts in a perforated plastic bag and freeze them in an airtight container. They should keep for 4 to 6 months. Once shelled, chestnuts will keep for 4 to 5 days if refrigerated and 9 to 12 months if frozen.

Chestnuts are traditionally roasted in their shells and peeled as they are eaten, but they're also delicious in sautés, stuffings, side dishes and baked desserts. Roasting chestnuts is simple. However, it is important to prepare chestnuts properly so they will peel easily. Wash chestnuts and soak in a bowl of cool water for 30 minutes. With a sharp knife, carefully make an incision in the shell across the center of the rounded sides of the chestnuts. Do not cut across the flat side.

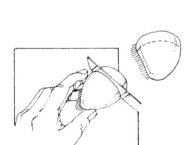

To roast chestnuts in a conventional oven, heat oven to 400°. Place chestnuts in a single layer on a baking sheet and roast for 20 to 30 minutes, stirring occasionally. Remove chestnuts from oven, cover with a dry cloth and cool for 5 minutes. Peel dark brown outer shell and bitter inner skin from nut and discard.

To roast chestnuts on an open fire, you'll need a chestnut pan, which is made of solid metal and has a series of dime-sized holes throughout the pan's bottom. Chestnut pans are imported from Italy and France and can be found in most kitchenware shops. Place chestnut pan over a gas flame or electric burner set on medium heat, or over hot coals. Distribute a single layer of soaked and slashed chestnuts in pan and roast for 20 to 30 minutes. Stir frequently to prevent nuts from burning. Peel dark brown outer shell and bitter inner skin from nut and discard.

BALSAMIC ROASTED ONIONS

Yield: about 3 cups

Serve these flavorful accompaniments with roasted pork, chicken or fish. These are also a popular and tasty pizza topping, especially when paired with roasted peppers. For an extra sweet, buttery flavor, use Vidalia onions. For a variation, use Spanish or red onions or a combination of different varieties.

6 medium Vidalia or yellow onions
5 tbs. canola or olive oil
2 tbs. balsamic vinegar
$\frac{1}{2}$ tsp. dried basil
1 tsp. dried thyme
salt and pepper to taste

Heat oven to 450°. Peel onions, keeping root end intact. Slice each onion into 6 wedges. In a small bowl, combine oil, vinegar, basil, thyme, salt and pepper and mix well. Place onion wedges snugly in an baking dish. Pour vinegar mixture over onions and cover with foil. Roast for 25 minutes. Remove foil, stir onions and roast uncovered for 10 minutes. Serve warm with remaining juices or reserve for another use.

ROASTED RED PEPPER SAUCE

Serve this sauce as an accompaniment to roasted foods.

2 medium red bell peppers, roasted (see page 8)
2 tbs. extra virgin olive oil
1 clove garlic
salt and pepper to taste

Puree all ingredients with a food processor or blender. Transfer to a small bowl and refrigerate until ready to use.

VARIATION: SPICY ROASTED RED PEPPER SAUCE

Add 2 roasted jalapeño peppers and an additional garlic clove to food processor.

ROASTED TOMATO SAUCE

To peel tomatoes, drop them into a pot of boiling water for 15 to 30 seconds, depending on ripeness. The skins will rub off easily. Use this sauce to accompany pasta with shrimp or chicken and as a topping for pizza.

8 large ripe tomatoes, peeled, cores removed
1 tbs. olive oil
2 tbs. dry white wine
1½ tbs. chopped fresh basil, or ½ tbs. dried
1 tbs. chopped fresh oregano, or 1 tsp. dried
½ tsp. freshly ground pepper
salt to taste

Heat oven to 425°. Place tomatoes in a large roasting pan and drizzle with olive oil and wine. Sprinkle with basil, oregano and pepper, cover and roast for 50 minutes. Remove from oven and cool for 10 to 15 minutes. Use a heavy potato masher to mash tomatoes. Return tomatoes to oven and roast for 20 minutes. Stir in salt if desired. Serve warm or cooled.

ROASTED GARLIC

Yield: ¼-⅓ cup

*Unless you have tasted roasted garlic, you probably erroneously assume it has the same pungency as raw garlic. Actually, by roasting, garlic's pungency mellows to a humble, succulent flavor with sweet, nutty undertones. Serve it in place of butter or soft cheese on crusty breads and crackers, or add it to dips, such as **Roasted Garlic Dipping Sauce**, page 29. A terra cotta garlic roaster is helpful, but not necessary.*

1 large bulb garlic
1 tbs. olive oil
⅛ tsp. dried basil or oregano
⅛ tsp. dried thyme
freshly ground pepper to taste

Heat oven to 350°. Cut ¼ inch from the top of garlic bulb and remove loose outer leaves; bulb should remain intact. Place bulb in a garlic roaster or on a sheet of aluminum foil. Pour olive oil over bulb and sprinkle with basil, thyme and pepper. Place lid on garlic roaster or wrap foil around bulb. For a medium to large bulb, roast for 50 minutes. For an extra-large bulb, roast for about 1 hour. Remove from oven and cool until able to handle. Separate cloves, squeeze out garlic pulp and discard skin.

ROASTED GARLIC OIL

Roasted garlic oil has a intriguing sweet flavor. The familiar pungency of raw garlic is transformed during the roasting process, and the oil becomes a delicate, mild and versatile ingredient. You can use roasted garlic oil in just about any recipe that calls for olive oil. The oil must be stored in the refrigerator and used the same day it's prepared.

6 large bulbs garlic
$\frac{1}{2}$ tsp. dried basil
$\frac{1}{2}$ tsp. dried thyme

$\frac{1}{8}$ tsp. freshly ground pepper
1 cup plus 1 tbs. olive oil

Roast garlic with basil, thyme, pepper and 1 tbs. of the olive oil according to instructions on page 15. Remove cover from garlic roaster or unwrap foil and roast for an additional 20 minutes. Cool until able to handle. Separate cloves, squeeze out garlic pulp and discard skins. In a medium bowl, combine 1 cup olive oil with roasted garlic pulp and mix well. Strain oil mixture through 3 to 4 layers of cheesecloth or a paper coffee filter. Squeeze cheesecloth or coffee filter to release flavored oil. Pour strained oil into a sterilized glass jar. Cover, refrigerate and use within 1 day.

ROASTED GARLIC PESTO

Making great-tasting pesto at home is a snap, and for home gardeners, it's a nice reward for tending to your own basil plants. Pesto is a natural choice for tossing with fresh pasta. But for a more exotic experience, place a few dollops of pesto on your next homemade pizza, or spread a layer of pesto over a fillet of fish or under the skin of a chicken before roasting.

1 bulb garlic, roasted (see page 15)
2 cups fresh basil leaves, firmly packed
¾ cup olive oil
¼ cup pine nuts or chopped walnuts
¼ tsp. freshly ground pepper
⅓ cup freshly grated Parmesan cheese
salt to taste

Combine garlic pulp, basil, olive oil, nuts and pepper in a food processor workbowl or blender container. Process for 15 to 20 seconds, until a paste forms. Pour into a bowl and stir in Parmesan cheese and salt.

ROASTED GARLIC AND SUN-DRIED TOMATO PESTO

In addition to tossing with pasta, serve this satisfying pesto as a dip or a spread on bruschetta or pita bread. It has incomparable flavor. Or, thin pesto with 2 tbs. hot water and spread it over roasted chicken, fish or pasta.

¼ cup dry sun-dried tomatoes
4 cloves garlic, roasted (see page 15)
¼ cup chopped fresh tomato
1 cup chopped broccoli, stems and
    florets, steamed until tender

½ cup olive oil
¼ cup pine nuts or chopped walnuts
⅛ tsp. freshly ground pepper
¼ cup grated Parmesan cheese
salt to taste

Rehydrate tomatoes in boiling water for 3 to 4 minutes or according to package directions; drain well and chop coarsely. Combine garlic pulp, sun-dried tomatoes, fresh tomato, broccoli, olive oil, nuts and pepper in a food processor workbowl or blender container. Process for 15 to 20 seconds, until a paste forms. Pour into a bowl stir in Parmesan cheese and salt.

ROASTED APPLE CHUNKS

Yield: about 2 cups

Roasting mellows and sweetens the tartness of fresh apples. Use them in breads, stuffings, muffins and cakes. Granny Smith or Red Delicious apples work well.

3 medium apples   ¼ cup canola oil

Heat oven to 400°. Peel, core and dice apples. Place apples in a small roasting pan and pour oil over apples. Roast for 25 minutes, until tender.

ROASTED APPLE SAUTÉ

Yield: about 3 cups

This works well as a side dish with roasted meats, such as veal, pork and ham. You can also add it to stuffings.

2 tbs. butter   2 cups *Roasted Apple Chunks*
1 large onion, chopped   6 tbs. maple syrup
2 stalks celery, thinly sliced   2 tbs. honey

Melt butter in a medium skillet over medium heat. Add onion and celery and sauté for 4 to 5 minutes. Add apples and sauté for 2 to 3 minutes. Stir in maple syrup and honey. Serve warm or cool for another use.

ROASTED CRANBERRY AND MANGO CHUTNEY

This freshly flavored and mildly spicy chutney has a very nice texture. You can store the extra chutney in the refrigerator for a couple of days and use it as a spread on cold poultry sandwiches. Or, serve it warm or at room temperature as a side dish for pork, poultry or lamb. Remove the seeds of the jalapeño for a milder chutney, or leave them in for a spicy kick.

1 tbs. olive oil
¾ cup sliced shallots
2 jalapeño peppers, finely chopped
1½ cups fresh cranberries
1 cup chopped, peeled mango
¾ cup orange juice

1 tbs. fresh lemon juice
1 tsp. grated fresh lemon peel (zest)
⅛ tsp. freshly ground pepper
¾ tsp. dried sage
salt to taste

Heat oven to 400°. In a medium bowl, combine all ingredients and mix well. Place mixture in a medium roasting pan and roast for 12 to 13 minutes, stirring occasionally. Remove from oven and transfer to a warm serving bowl. Or, cool completely and refrigerate.

OVEN-ROASTED BERRY CHUTNEY

Yield: about 4 cups

This exciting, quick and easy chutney makes cooking a joy, not a chore. Serve it with fresh bread or water crackers, or with roasted meats, poultry or fish.

1 cup fresh blueberries
25 fresh strawberries, hulled
juice from 1 lemon
2 tbs. butter, melted
½ tsp. grated ginger root
1 tbs. raspberry vinegar
1 tsp. sugar
1 tbs. chopped fresh basil
½ cup finely chopped walnuts

Heat oven to 400°. Place blueberries and strawberries, hulled-side down, in a medium roasting pan. Drizzle with 2 tbs. of the lemon juice, and melted butter. Roast for 7 to 8 minutes until strawberries are tender. Remove from oven and cool. Halve strawberries. In a medium bowl, combine strawberry halves, blueberries and pan juices with remaining lemon juice, ginger, vinegar, sugar, basil and walnuts. Mix well and cool. Serve cold or at room temperature.

APPETIZERS AND SNACKS

HONEY-ROASTED PEANUTS AND POPCORN

It's wise to invest in a good-quality oven thermometer to test the accuracy of your oven's temperature.

½ cup unsalted peanuts
2 tbs. honey
½ tsp. salt
9 cups plain popped popcorn

6 tbs. maple syrup
3 tbs. unsalted butter
3 tbs. brown sugar

Heat oven to 400°. In a small bowl, combine peanuts, honey and salt and mix until well coated. Spread peanut mixture in a single layer on a nonstick baking sheet. Roast for 8 minutes, remove from oven and transfer to a shallow bowl. Cool. Separate peanuts. Reduce oven heat to 250°. Lightly coat a large baking sheet with nonstick cooking spray. Spread popcorn evenly on sheet. In a small saucepan, combine syrup, butter and brown sugar. Heat over medium-high heat for 2 to 3 minutes, stirring constantly, until bubbling. Pour mixture over popcorn and mix with a wooden spoon quickly and thoroughly, until popcorn is well coated. Sprinkle popcorn with roasted peanuts and roast for about 20 minutes. Remove from oven, pour into a large serving bowl and cool. Break any large clumps into bite-sized pieces.

SPICY ROASTED PITA CHIPS

Once you taste these chips, you're hooked. They're loaded with flavor and go great with dips and salsas, but can easily stand on their own. To maintain freshness, store the chips in an airtight container.

½ cup olive or canola oil
½ tsp. cayenne pepper
¼ tsp. freshly ground black pepper
¼ tsp. onion powder
2 tsp. chili powder
½ tsp. dry mustard
1 tsp. red pepper flakes
4 loaves pita bread

Heat oven to 375°. In a small bowl, whisk together oil, cayenne and black pepper, onion powder, chili powder, mustard and red pepper flakes. Split open pita pockets and cut in half to make 4 half-moon shapes per pita. Lay pita slices with the rough side up and brush entire surface with oil mixture. Roast for 10 minutes, remove from oven and cool. Break into 2-inch pieces and serve warm or at room temperature.

ROASTED MIXED NUTS

Absolutely delicious! Just about any kind of nut will work in this tasty snack. Their flavor is lively, yet they're surprisingly easy to make. Pack the flavored nuts in a covered glass jar, tied with a ribbon, for a special holiday gift.

1½ cups pecans, large pieces or halves
1¾ cups whole almonds
¾ cup walnuts, large pieces or halves
1 egg white
½ cup sugar
2 tbs. cinnamon
¼ tsp. nutmeg
⅛ tsp. ground allspice
⅛ tsp. ground cloves

Heat oven to 300°. In a large bowl, combine nuts and egg white; mix well. In a separate bowl, mix together sugar, cinnamon, nutmeg, allspice and cloves. Add spice mixture to nut mixture and mix thoroughly until nuts are well coated. Spread nuts on a nonstick or parchment paper-lined baking sheet and roast for 30 minutes, stirring occasionally. Cool.

ROASTED SUN-DRIED TOMATO AND SPINACH SPREAD

Serve this spread on fresh vegetables, crackers, chips, calzones or seafood. For a colorful and tasty combination, increase the oil by ¼ cup and double the lemon juice. Mix with cold pasta or toss with bite-sized pieces of roasted chicken. Be sure to wash and dry spinach thoroughly before using. It often has sand particles clinging to the leaves, even if the package says it's prewashed.

1 cup dry sun-dried tomatoes
2 tsp. plus 3 tbs. extra virgin olive oil
¼ cup pine nuts
¼ cup chopped walnuts
1 lb. fresh spinach, stems removed
1 cup fresh basil leaves, firmly packed
2 cloves garlic, minced or pressed
⅛ tsp. freshly ground pepper
salt to taste
1 tsp. fresh lemon juice
¼ cup freshly grated Parmesan cheese

Heat oven to 400°. Rehydrate sun-dried tomatoes in boiling water for 3 to 4 minutes or according to package directions; drain well and chop coarsely. Toss sun-dried tomatoes with 2 tsp. olive oil in a small bowl until coated. Spread sun-dried tomatoes on a nonstick baking sheet and roast for 10 minutes, stirring occasionally. Remove from oven and set aside.

Spread pine nuts in a single layer on a nonstick baking sheet and roast for 2 minutes; remove from oven and set aside. Spread walnuts in a single layer on a nonstick baking sheet and roast for 6 minutes; remove from oven and set aside.

Place spinach in a large, dry pot over medium heat and cook until just wilted, about 3 to 5 minutes.

Combine all ingredients, except cheese, in a food processor workbowl. Process for 15 to 20 seconds or until a paste forms. Pour into a bowl and mix in Parmesan cheese. Refrigerate until ready to serve.

SANTA FE ROASTED BEAN DIP

Yield: 2 cups

*This is a very popular dish for a hot or cold buffet. Serve it with **Spicy Roasted Pita Chips**, page 24, or raw vegetables. This enticing dip can be prepared a day or two in advance — just keep it covered and refrigerated.*

3 cloves garlic
1 large white onion, cut into 6 wedges
    (do not separate layers)
½ cup olive oil
1 can (14 oz.) garbanzo beans, rinsed,
    drained
1 can (14 oz.) cannellini (white kidney)
    beans, rinsed, drained
2 jalapeño peppers, roasted (see page 8)

2 tbs. fresh lemon juice
2½ tbs. fresh lime juice
1½ tbs. chili powder
1 tsp. ground cumin
⅛ tsp. cayenne pepper
salt to taste
2 tbs. chopped fresh cilantro leaves
1 sprig fresh cilantro for garnish

Heat oven to 450°. Place garlic and onion in a small roasting pan and toss with 2 tbs. of the olive oil. Cover and roast for 25 minutes. Uncover and roast for 5 minutes. Cool. With a food processor or blender, puree beans until smooth. Add jalapeños, lemon and lime juice, chili powder, cumin, cayenne and salt and process until just blended. Slowly add remaining olive oil and process until well blended. Transfer bean dip to a serving bowl and stir in chopped cilantro. Garnish with a sprig of cilantro.

ROASTED GARLIC DIPPING SAUCE

Yield: 1 cup

Serve this scrumptious dipping sauce with assorted fresh vegetables, crackers or chips.

1 bulb garlic, roasted (see page 15)
½ cup plain nonfat yogurt
½ cup mayonnaise
1 tbs. chopped fresh chives
⅛ tsp. salt
⅛ tsp. freshly ground pepper

Mash garlic pulp and combine with yogurt, mayonnaise, chives, salt and pepper. Mix well. Refrigerate for at least 3 hours before serving. Serve chilled.

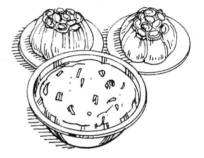

ROASTED GARLIC HUMMUS

Yield: 2 cups

Hummus is a Middle Eastern dip or spread that's traditionally served as an appetizer or snack. You can prepare our roasted garlic version up to 2 days in advance — just keep it covered and refrigerated. Serve chilled with pieces of fresh pita bread or try it with **Spicy Roasted Pita Chips**, *page 24. Tahini, or sesame seed paste, can be found in health food stores, specialty food stores and many grocery stores.*

1 bulb garlic, roasted (see page 15)
1 can (14 oz.) garbanzo beans, rinsed, drained
1/4 cup tahini (sesame seed paste)
2 tbs. water
1 tbs. olive oil

1 tsp. chili powder
1/8 tsp. ground cumin
1/4 tsp. freshly ground pepper
1/8 tsp. salt
1/8 tsp. paprika, optional

Combine garlic pulp with garbanzo beans, tahini, water, olive oil, chili powder, cumin, pepper and salt in a food processor workbowl and process for 4 minutes, until smooth. Transfer mixture to a serving bowl and sprinkle with paprika, if desired. Refrigerate for at least 2 hours before serving.

ROASTED VEGETABLE SALSA

Yield: 2 cups

*Pair this intensely flavored salsa with **Spicy Roasted Pita Chips**, page 24, for a delicious and impressive appetizer or snack. For a fabulous alternative, we like to spread a layer of this salsa over roasted chicken or swordfish.*

1 small red onion, coarsely chopped
1 small white onion, coarsely chopped
1 tsp. olive oil
½ bulb garlic, roasted (see page 15)
2 jalapeño peppers, roasted (see page 8), finely chopped
½ medium red bell pepper, roasted (see page 8), finely chopped

½ medium green bell pepper, roasted (see page 8), finely chopped
1 can (1 lb. 12 oz.) crushed tomatoes in puree
1 tbs. chili powder
⅛ tsp. ground cumin
2 tsp. fresh lemon juice
salt to taste

Heat oven to 450°. In a small bowl, combine onions and oil. Place onions in a small roasting pan and roast for 20 minutes, stirring occasionally. Cool and set aside. Combine all ingredients in a medium bowl and mix well. For best flavor, refrigerate salsa for at least 4 hours or overnight.

ROASTED EGGPLANT AND CHUNKY TOMATO CROSTINI

This no-hassle, picture-pretty appetizer takes less than 20 minutes to prepare and is a super way to use up day-old bread. It's wonderful warm or chilled.

14-16 slices Italian bread, ¼-inch thick
¼ cup extra virgin olive oil
2 cloves garlic, halved
8 slices eggplant, ½-inch thick
4 plum tomatoes, seeded, chopped

1 tbs. balsamic vinegar
4 fresh basil leaves, chopped
salt to taste
grated Parmesan cheese for garnish,
   optional

Brush both sides of each slice of bread with olive oil. Toast bread on both sides in a toaster oven or under a broiler. Rub one side of each slice of toast with cut sides of garlic.

Heat oven to 425°. Place eggplant slices on a lightly greased baking sheet and brush with olive oil. Roast for 10 minutes, remove from oven and cool. Cut eggplant slices into ½-inch cubes. In a medium bowl, combine eggplant, tomatoes, remaining olive oil, vinegar, chopped basil and salt and mix well. Top each slice of toasted bread with equal portions of eggplant-tomato mixture. Garnish with Parmesan cheese if desired.

ROASTED MUSHROOM CAPS

Servings: 2

Serve this as a side dish or spoon over slices of toasted Italian bread for a luscious bruschetta. You can find a mushroom brush at most kitchenware shops. For a variation, substitute other varieties of mushrooms.

12 large white mushrooms
1/4 cup pine nuts
2 cloves garlic, minced or pressed
1 tbs. fresh lemon juice
1 tbs. freshly grated Parmesan cheese

1/8 tsp. salt
1/4 tsp. freshly ground pepper
2 tbs. butter, melted
1 tbs. olive oil
1/2 tsp. finely chopped fresh parsley

Heat oven to 375°. Wipe mushrooms clean with a damp cloth or mushroom brush. Remove stems and set caps aside. Cut 1/4 inch from stems and discard. Chop remaining stems finely and combine in a bowl with pine nuts, garlic, lemon juice, Parmesan cheese, salt and pepper. Lay mushroom caps, stem-side up, in a small ovenproof dish. Divide pine nut mixture among mushroom caps and drizzle with butter and oil. Roast for 15 minutes, remove from oven and sprinkle with parsley. Serve warm.

ROASTED PORTOBELLO MUSHROOMS WITH SPICY RED PEPPER SAUCE

Servings: 4

This treasured mushroom appetizer has an outstanding combination of flavors. The versatile presentation suits any occasion, from formal to casual. If you can't find a Vidalia onion, use Maui, Walla Walla or another sweet, mild onion.

½ lb. portobello mushrooms
1 large Vidalia onion, thinly sliced, layers separated
½ tsp. dried oregano
salt to taste
6 tbs. olive oil
Spicy Roasted Red Pepper Sauce, page 13
sliced Italian or French bread

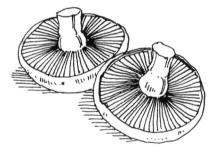

Heat oven to 450°. Wipe mushrooms clean with a damp cloth or mushroom brush, remove stems and discard. Slice mushroom caps into ½-inch strips. In a large bowl, combine mushroom strips, onion, oregano, salt and olive oil. Mix until vegetables are well coated. Place mushroom mixture in a large roasting pan and roast for 20 minutes, stirring occasionally.

Warm red pepper sauce in a small saucepan over low heat until heated through. Place equal amounts of pepper sauce on individual serving plates. Top sauce with equal amounts of roasted mushroom mixture and serve with sliced Italian or French bread.

CAJUN CHICKEN WINGS

This recipe takes chicken wings to a new level. Your portable electric roaster or conventional oven will produce professional results.

1-1¼ lb. chicken wings, about 6
½ tbs. hot paprika
½ tbs. onion powder
½ tbs. garlic powder
½ tbs. black pepper
½ tsp. dried thyme

½ tsp. dried oregano
¼ tsp. cayenne pepper
½ tsp. chili powder
salt to taste
¼ cup olive oil

Remove excess skin from wings, rinse and pat dry. Combine remaining ingredients in a bowl and mix well. Add chicken wings and toss to coat with marinade. Marinate chicken wings overnight, covered, in the refrigerator.

Heat a 6-quart roaster oven to 425°. Or, heat a conventional oven to 450°. Place chicken wings with marinade on a baking sheet. Roast for 40 to 45 minutes or until wings are no longer pink in the center.

ROASTED PEEL-AND-EAT SHRIMP

Servings: 4-6

Roasting locks in the distinctive, succulent flavor of the shrimp. This is an irresistible appetizer for a leisurely social occasion. Provide lots of napkins and a large bowl to discard shrimp shells as they are peeled.

1 lb. large shrimp, unpeeled, legs removed
1 cup olive oil
4 cloves garlic, coarsely minced
$\frac{1}{2}$ tsp. dried basil
1 tsp. dried parsley
1 lemon, cut into wedges

Rinse shrimp and dry thoroughly. Combine all ingredients in a large bowl; mix well and refrigerate overnight.

Heat oven to 450°. Place all ingredients in a medium roasting pan and roast for 5 minutes. Set oven control to broil and broil shrimp for 2 minutes. Discard marinade. Serve shrimp with fresh lemon wedges.

OVEN-ROASTED VEGETABLE SANDWICH

Servings: 2

You can bring the outdoor flavor of crunchy grilled vegetables indoors with this easy-to-assemble recipe. It's delicious year-round, served on lightly toasted French bread. For an extra treat, sprinkle 2 tbs. freshly grated Parmesan cheese over the roasted vegetables.

1 clove garlic, minced or pressed
1/2 tsp. dry mustard
1/2 tbs. fresh lemon juice
3 tbs. balsamic vinegar
5 tbs. olive oil
1 tbs. chopped fresh basil, or 1 tsp. dried
1/8 tsp. freshly ground pepper
6-8 slices eggplant, 1/4-inch thick

1/2 medium red bell pepper, cut into
  1/2-inch strips
1 medium carrot, cut lengthwise into
  6-8 slices
1 medium zucchini, cut into 1/4-inch
  rounds
1 small red onion, cut into 1/8-inch circles
4 slices toasted French bread

Combine garlic, dry mustard, lemon juice, vinegar, oil, basil and pepper in a bowl and whisk together. In a large bowl, combine vegetables with marinade. Mix well, cover and refrigerate for 2 hours.

Heat oven to 425°. Place vegetables with marinade on a baking sheet and roast for 20 minutes, turning occasionally. Heat broiler and broil vegetables for 3 minutes. Serve warm between slices of toasted bread.

ROASTED SESAME PORK ROLL-UPS

Servings: 2

Sesame oil adds a familiar Asian flavor to the pork. The oil is highly flavored, so it's only used sparingly to flavor foods.

1 tbs. sesame seeds
1 lb. boneless pork loin, cut into ¼-inch strips
¼ cup low-sodium soy sauce
1 clove garlic, minced or pressed
3-4 drops sesame oil
two 8-inch flour or whole wheat tortillas
shredded romaine lettuce

Heat oven to 400°. Sprinkle sesame seeds on a baking sheet and toast for 3 to 4 minutes or until golden brown, stirring occasionally. In a medium bowl, combine pork strips, sesame seeds, soy sauce and garlic. Marinate pork in the refrigerator for 2 hours.

Heat oven to 425°. Place pork strips on a baking sheet and roast for 20 minutes, basting occasionally with marinade. Remove roasted pork from oven and place in a clean bowl. Discard marinade. Drizzle pork with sesame oil and mix well. Spread roasted pork evenly on 2 tortillas. Cover pork with shredded lettuce and roll up into a cylinder. Serve immediately.

ROASTED PEPPER AND ONION PIZZA

Servings: 3-4

We created a cheeseless pizza with such a delightful array of toppings that you won't even miss the cheese. If desired, you can use a bread machine, food processor or heavy duty mixer to make the dough.

1 pkg. active dry yeast
1 cup plus 1 tbs. warm water
1 tbs. sugar
3$\frac{1}{4}$ cups all-purpose flour
$\frac{1}{2}$ tsp. salt
3 tbs. olive oil
cornmeal
$\frac{1}{2}$ cup fresh arugula leaves, torn into 1$\frac{1}{2}$-inch pieces
1 tsp. balsamic vinegar
1 tsp. olive oil
2 medium red or green bell peppers, roasted (see page 8), cut into $\frac{1}{2}$-inch strips
$\frac{3}{4}$ cup sliced *Balsamic Roasted Onions*, page 12
1 cup tomato-based pizza sauce
$\frac{1}{2}$ tsp. dried basil
$\frac{1}{4}$ tsp. dried oregano
salt to taste

In a small bowl, dissolve yeast in water and add sugar. Set aside for 5 minutes. In a large bowl, mix flour with salt. Add yeast mixture and olive oil to flour mixture and stir together to form a ball. Place dough on a floured surface and knead for 10 minutes. Place dough in a greased bowl and cover with a towel or plastic wrap. Let rise for 1½ hours in a warm, draft-free area. Punch down dough and let rest for 10 minutes. Roll out dough to fit a 14-inch pizza pan or baking stone sprinkled with cornmeal.

Heat oven to 425°. In a small bowl, combine arugula, vinegar and ½ tsp. of the olive oil. Mix well and set aside. Spread pizza sauce evenly over dough. Distribute peppers and onions over sauce and sprinkle with basil, oregano and salt. Drizzle topping with remaining ½ tsp. olive oil. Bake for 25 minutes or until crust is lightly browned. Remove from oven and distribute arugula on cooked pizza. Slice pizza and serve immediately.

HERBED FLATBREAD STUFFED WITH ROASTED VEGETABLES

This makes a perfect first course for a traditional Italian dinner featuring fresh pasta with seafood, veal or poultry in a red sauce. The bread can be served hot or cold.

1 pkg. active dry yeast
1 cup plus 1 tbs. warm water
1 tbs. sugar
3¼ cups all-purpose flour
½ tsp. salt
3 tbs. olive oil
3 large tomatoes, sliced ⅛-inch thick
2 medium-sized sweet onions, sliced ⅛-inch thick
2 medium zucchini, sliced ¼-inch thick
¼ cup olive oil
1 tsp. dried thyme
½ tsp. red pepper flakes
⅛ tsp. freshly ground pepper
1 cup shredded low-fat mozzarella cheese

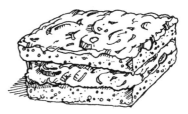

In a small bowl, dissolve yeast in water and add sugar. Set aside for 5 minutes. In a large bowl, mix flour with salt. Add yeast mixture and 3 tbs. olive oil and stir together to form a ball. Place dough on a floured surface and knead for 10 minutes. Place dough in a greased bowl and cover with a towel or plastic wrap. Let rise for 1½ hours in a warm, draft-free area. Punch down dough and let rest for 10 minutes.

Heat oven to 425°. While dough is rising, place tomato, onion and zucchini slices on a lightly greased baking sheet. Drizzle with ¼ cup olive oil and sprinkle with thyme, red pepper flakes and pepper. Roast for 12 minutes. Remove from oven and set aside.

Divide dough into 2 halves. Roll out each half to fit a greased 8½-x-12-inch baking pan. Place 1 piece of the dough in pan, pressing and stretching so it extends to all sides. Spread ½ of the cheese on top, followed by ½ of the vegetables. Top with remaining dough, stretching so it extends to all sides. Top with remaining cheese and vegetables. Roast for 25 minutes. Heat broiler and broil for 2 to 3 minutes, until cheese is bubbly and bread is lightly browned. Cut into medium-sized square pieces and serve hot or at room temperature.

FOCACCIA WITH ROASTED EGGPLANT AND TOMATOES

There's something about the flavor and aroma of great focaccia that makes it hard to resist. You can serve this as an appetizer for a small group, or divide it in half and you've got dinner for two.

1 pkg. active dry yeast
1 cup plus 1 tbs. water
1 tbs. sugar
3¼ cups all-purpose flour
½ tsp. salt
3 tbs. olive oil
2 cloves garlic, minced
8-10 slices eggplant, ⅛-inch thick
8-10 slices tomato, ⅛-inch thick
2 tbs. olive oil
2 tbs. balsamic vinegar
½ tsp. dried basil
¼ tsp. dried oregano
salt to taste
½ cup freshly grated Parmesan cheese

In a small bowl, dissolve yeast in water and add sugar. Set aside for 5 minutes. In a large bowl, mix flour with salt. Add yeast mixture and 3 tbs. olive oil and stir together to form a ball. Place dough on a floured surface and knead for 10 minutes. Place dough in a greased bowl and cover with a towel or plastic wrap. Let rise for 1½ hours in a warm, draft-free area. Punch down dough and let rest for 10 minutes.

Heat oven to 425°. Place garlic, eggplant and tomato slices in a metal roasting pan. In a small bowl, mix together 2 tbs. olive oil, vinegar, basil, oregano and salt. Pour over vegetables in roasting pan and roast for 10 minutes, turning once. Remove from oven and set aside.

Reduce oven heat to 400°. Roll out dough to fit a 10-inch round pizza pan or pie plate. Spray pan with cooking spray and place dough in pan. Top dough with cheese and roasted vegetables and bake for 25 minutes. Cut into serving pieces and serve hot or at room temperature.

ROASTED GARLIC BREAD

This popular snack has just the right combination of ingredients. Indulge and serve this amazingly aromatic and tasty garlic bread with your next gourmet Italian feast.

2 bulbs garlic, roasted (see page 15)
1 tbs. extra virgin olive oil
2 tbs. freshly grated Parmesan or Romano cheese
3/4 tsp. dried basil
1/4 tsp. dried oregano
1/4 tsp. freshly ground pepper
1/8 tsp. salt
1 loaf Italian or French bread

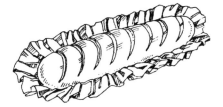

Heat oven to 375°. Mash garlic pulp, if necessary, to form a paste. Combine garlic paste with olive oil, cheese, basil, oregano, pepper and salt. Mix thoroughly. Slice bread at an angle at 1-inch intervals, leaving loaf intact at the bottom. Spread garlic mixture between bread slices. Wrap bread in foil and bake for 20 minutes. Serve warm.

ROASTED APPLE AND WALNUT BREAD

Yield: 2 small loaves

This thick-crusted bread has a rich, natural flavor and rustic texture. It's superb for breakfast, dinner and picnics, and makes a nice gift. To toast walnuts, place them on a nonstick or parchment-lined baking sheet in a preheated 375° oven for 9 minutes, shaking occasionally. Remove from oven and cool.

1 pkg. active dry yeast
1 cup warm milk (100°-110°)
1 tbs. sugar
1½ cups whole wheat flour
1 cup all-purpose flour

1 tsp. salt
¼ cup canola oil
1 cup walnuts, toasted
1 Granny Smith apple, diced, roasted
(see page 19)

In a small bowl, dissolve yeast in milk and add sugar. Set aside for 5 minutes. In a large bowl, combine flours, salt, oil and yeast mixture. Stir together to form a ball. Place dough on a floured surface and knead for 10 minutes. Place dough in a greased bowl, cover with a towel or plastic wrap and let rise for 1 to 1½ hours in a warm, draft-free area. Punch down dough and knead in toasted walnuts and roasted apples. Form dough into a ball, cover with a towel or plastic wrap and let rise for 30 minutes. Divide dough into 2 halves and form each half into a round loaf. Place loaves on a lightly greased baking sheet and bake for 30 minutes, until crust is golden brown. Remove from oven and cool on a wire rack.

SOUPS AND SALADS

ROASTED VEGETABLE SOUP

This refreshing, aromatic soup has an intriguing roasted vegetable flavor. Serve in individual soup bowls with slices of freshly baked bread or rolls.

1 medium eggplant, peeled, cut into ½-inch cubes
1 large red bell pepper, cut into ¼-inch strips
1 large red onion, peeled, cut into 8 wedges
2 stalks celery, chopped
2 medium zucchini, cut into ¼-inch rounds

1½ cups mushrooms, halved
3 tbs. olive oil
¼ cup balsamic vinegar
2 cloves garlic, minced or pressed
6 cups beef stock
2 tbs. low-sodium soy sauce
½ tsp. dried thyme
¾ tsp. dried marjoram
salt and pepper to taste

Heat oven to 425°. In a large bowl, combine eggplant, pepper, onion, celery, zucchini, mushrooms, 2 tbs. of the olive oil, and balsamic vinegar. Mix thoroughly. Arrange vegetables in a medium roasting pan or baking sheet. Roast vegetables for 25 minutes, stirring occasionally. Remove from oven and set aside. Heat 1 tbs. of the olive oil in a large stockpot. Add garlic and sauté over medium heat for 2 to 3 minutes or until just golden. Add beef stock, soy sauce and herbs. Add roasted vegetables and stir well. Bring to a boil, reduce heat and simmer for 2 to 3 hours.

ROASTED CARROT AND POTATO SOUP

Servings: 4

Pureed roasted vegetables infuse soup stock with a subtle roasted accent that's delicious hot or cold. It makes a nice lunch when paired with a garden salad. Or, use it as a starter for a special dining event.

6 carrots, cut into $1\frac{1}{2}$-inch pieces
1 lb. red-skinned potatoes, cut into $1\frac{1}{4}$-inch cubes
1 large Vidalia or other sweet onion, quartered, layers separated
3 cloves garlic
2 tbs. olive oil
$3\frac{1}{2}$ cups chicken stock
1 tbs. fresh lemon juice
1 tbs. honey
$\frac{1}{4}$ tsp. ground cloves
$\frac{1}{4}$ tsp. ground ginger
salt and pepper to taste
$\frac{1}{2}$ cup milk
chopped fresh chives for garnish, optional

Heat oven to 400°. In a large bowl, toss carrots, potatoes, onion and garlic with olive oil until well coated. Place all vegetables in a medium roasting pan or baking sheet and roast for 30 to 35 minutes or until tender when pierced with a fork. Remove from oven and cool. When cool enough to handle, process vegetables with a food processor or blender until smooth.

In a large stockpot, heat chicken stock over medium heat. Add lemon juice, honey, cloves, ginger, salt, pepper and milk and stir well. Whisk in pureed vegetables and heat through. Serve immediately in individual soup bowls, or cool to room temperature, chill in the refrigerator and serve chilled. Garnish with chopped fresh chives if desired.

ROASTED ONION AND GARLIC SOUP

Servings: 2

The sweet and savory flavors of this recipe come together beautifully. Serve it as an appetizer for an elegant meal, or pair it with a salad and rolls for a soothing lunch.

5 tbs. olive oil
2 tbs. balsamic vinegar
2 tsp. dried thyme
salt and pepper to taste
5 medium Vidalia or other sweet onions, cut into $\frac{1}{8}$-inch slices
1 bulb garlic, roasted (see page 15)
8 cups beef stock
1 tbs. Worcestershire sauce
croutons for garnish, optional
grated Swiss cheese for garnish, optional

Heat oven to 450°. In a small bowl, combine oil, vinegar, thyme, salt and pepper. Place onion slices in an ovenproof dish. Pour vinegar mixture over onions and cover with foil. Roast for 15 minutes. Remove foil, stir onions and roast uncovered for 8 to 10 minutes.

Squeeze roasted garlic from each clove into a food processor workbowl or blender container and puree until smooth. Combine beef stock, Worcestershire sauce and pureed garlic in a large saucepan or stockpot. Add onions and simmer for 45 to 55 minutes. Serve in individual ovenproof soup bowls topped with croutons and Swiss cheese, if using. Place under the broiler for 1 to 2 minutes until cheese is bubbly and golden brown.

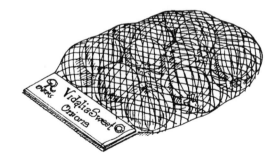

LOW-FAT CREAMY ROASTED TOMATO SOUP

Servings: 4

This recipe offers luxurious, restaurant-quality richness, yet it's made in your own kitchen. It's also low in fat and easy to prepare. Roasting allows the tomatoes and shallots to develop a lively and complex flavor that's truly outstanding. Serve the soup warm as a first course or pair with a fresh garden salad and dinner rolls for a light meal.

6 large ripe tomatoes, peeled, cores removed
2 shallots, chopped
2 tbs. olive oil
3½ cups nonfat (skim) milk
3 tbs. flour
¾ tsp. dried basil
½ tsp. dried oregano
¼ tsp. freshly ground pepper
salt to taste

Heat oven to 425°. Place tomatoes and shallots in a large roasting pan and drizzle with olive oil. Cover and roast for 50 minutes. Remove from oven and cool for 10 to 15 minutes. Puree roasted tomatoes and shallots with a food processor or blender until smooth.

In a large saucepan, whisk together milk and flour. Add pureed tomato mixture, basil, oregano, pepper and salt. Cover partially and cook over medium-low heat for 30 minutes. Serve hot in individual soup bowls.

Note: To peel tomatoes, plunge them in a pot of boiling water for 15 to 30 seconds, depending on ripeness. Peel skin with a small sharp knife or your fingers.

ROASTED EGGPLANT SALAD
WITH BALSAMIC BASIL VINAIGRETTE

The distinctive flavors in this dish complement each other nicely and the color contrast is beautiful. You can serve this dish on individual serving plates or a large serving platter.

4 small Japanese eggplants, cut lengthwise into $\frac{1}{2}$-inch slices
1 medium red onion, thinly sliced, layers separated
6 tbs. extra virgin olive oil
1 medium red bell pepper, roasted (see page 8)
1 medium yellow bell pepper, roasted (see page 8)
3 tbs. balsamic vinegar
1 tbs. fresh lemon juice
$\frac{1}{8}$ tsp. dry mustard
1 clove garlic, minced or pressed
8 fresh basil leaves, finely chopped
2 tbs. sliced black olives
$\frac{1}{4}$ cup crumbled feta or goat cheese

Heat oven to 450°. Place eggplant slices and onion rings in a large roasting pan or baking sheet and drizzle with 2 tbs. of the olive oil. Roast for 15 to 17 minutes, until lightly browned. Remove from oven and cool. Slice roasted peppers into ¼-inch strips. On a large serving platter, arrange eggplant slices, onions and roasted pepper strips. In a small bowl, whisk together remaining olive oil, balsamic vinegar, lemon juice, dry mustard, garlic and basil. Drizzle vinaigrette over eggplant, onions and peppers. Top with black olives and crumbled cheese. Serve immediately.

ROASTED EGGPLANT AND ORZO SALAD WITH LEMON HERB VINAIGRETTE

Servings: 6

Orzo is a neglected rice-shaped pasta that works well in vegetable and pasta combination dishes.

VINAIGRETTE

¼ cup fresh lemon juice
½ cup olive oil
1½ tsp. grated fresh lemon peel (zest)
1½ tbs. finely chopped fresh parsley

¾ tbs. finely chopped fresh basil
⅛ tsp. salt
⅛ tsp. freshly ground pepper
½ tsp. dry mustard

SALAD

⅓ cup walnut pieces
4½-6 qt. water
½ tsp. plus ⅛ tsp. salt
¼ tsp. plus 1½ tbs. olive oil
1 pkg. (16 oz.) orzo

2 small eggplants, diced
1 tbs. red pepper flakes
1 small red onion, quartered, layers
    separated
⅛ tsp. freshly ground pepper
salt to taste

For vinaigrette, whisk together all ingredients in a small bowl. Set aside.

For salad, heat oven to 350°. Spread walnuts in a single layer on a baking sheet and toast for 8 minutes. Cool. In a large pot, bring water to a boil. Add ½ tsp. salt and ¼ tsp. olive oil. Add orzo and cook until just tender, about 8 to 10 minutes, stirring occasionally. Pour off water, rinse and drain thoroughly.

Increase oven heat to 375°. In a medium bowl, combine eggplant, 1½ lbs. olive oil, red pepper flakes, red onion, ⅛ tsp. salt and freshly ground pepper. Mix thoroughly. Arrange vegetables in a metal roasting pan and roast for 30 minutes, stirring occasionally. Remove from oven and cool. In a medium bowl, combine cooked orzo, roasted vegetables, toasted walnuts and vinaigrette. Mix thoroughly and serve.

ROASTED RED POTATO SALAD

Servings: 4

Here's a no-fuss, time-saving salad that goes exceptionally well with poultry or seafood. It can be prepared in advance, making it an ideal addition to your buffet table.

1 lb. small red-skinned potatoes
1 medium red onion, chopped
½ cup extra virgin olive oil
2 celery stalks, finely chopped
2 tbs. balsamic vinegar
2 scallions, finely chopped
salt and pepper to taste
½ tsp. sweet paprika

Heat oven to 400°. Cut potatoes into 1- to 1¼-inch cubes. Place potatoes and red onion in a medium roasting pan and toss with 2 tbs. of the olive oil until well coated. Roast for 20 to 25 minutes or until potatoes are tender when pierced with a fork. Remove from oven and cool. Combine all ingredients in a large bowl and mix well. Serve at room temperature or chilled.

ROASTED CHICKEN SALAD

*This makes a luxurious, low-fat and fresh-tasting lunch for two. It has a mild smoky flavor. Use leftover **Balsamic Dijon Chicken**, page 88, **Favorite Roasted Chicken**, page 90, **Vertically Roasted Garlic Chicken**, page 91, or any other cooked chicken.*

6 tbs. plain low-fat yogurt
$\frac{1}{2}$ tsp. dry mustard
$\frac{1}{2}$ tsp. balsamic vinegar
$1\frac{1}{2}$ tbs. *Roasted Red Pepper Sauce*, page 13
1 lb. roasted chicken meat, cut into $\frac{1}{2}$-inch strips
2 tbs. finely chopped red bell pepper
2 tbs. finely chopped celery
2 tbs. finely chopped red onion
salt and pepper to taste
2 leaves romaine or red leaf lettuce

In a small bowl, combine yogurt, dry mustard, vinegar and *Roasted Red Pepper Sauce* and mix well. In a medium bowl, mix chicken with red pepper, celery, onion, salt and pepper. Add yogurt mixture and mix well. Place lettuce leaves on individual serving plates. Arrange chicken mixture on top of lettuce and serve immediately.

ROASTED SESAME CHICKEN SALAD

Servings: 4

Instead of roasting a whole chicken, you can substitute 4 to 5 cups leftover roasted chicken or turkey meat.

3 tbs. butter, melted
2 tsp. fresh lemon juice
2½ lb. chicken
⅛ tsp. salt
¼ tsp. freshly ground pepper
⅓ tsp. dried basil
⅓ tsp. dried thyme
½ lemon
2 tbs. sesame seeds
1 head romaine lettuce, shredded
1 head iceberg lettuce, shredded
1 medium red bell pepper, cut into small strips
1 medium yellow bell pepper, cut into small strips
3 tbs. white wine vinegar
2 tbs. low-sodium soy sauce
⅛ tsp. sesame oil

Heat oven to 325°. Combine melted butter and lemon juice in a small bowl and set aside. Remove giblets from chicken and discard. Rinse chicken and pat dry. Rub chicken with lemon-butter mixture. Season chicken cavity and sprinkle chicken with salt, pepper, basil and thyme. Insert ½ lemon in cavity of chicken. Truss chicken loosely (see page 3). Place chicken breast-side up on a nonstick or liberally oiled roasting rack in a roasting pan. Roast for about 1½ hours, basting every 12 to 15 minutes with remaining lemon-butter mixture, until a thermometer reads 170° when inserted in breast, or until juices run clear when thickest part of breast is pierced with a knife. Remove chicken from oven and transfer to a serving platter, breast-side up. Cover with foil or parchment paper and let sit for 15 minutes. When cool enough to handle, remove chicken from bones and break into bite-sized pieces.

Increase oven heat to 400°. Spread sesame seeds on a nonstick baking sheet and toast for 3 to 4 minutes or until golden brown. In a large bowl, toss together chicken, romaine, iceberg lettuce, red and yellow peppers, vinegar, soy sauce, sesame seeds and sesame oil. Serve warm or chilled.

SIDE DISHES

ROASTED GARLIC MASHED POTATOES

These are absolutely the best tasting mashed potatoes we have ever had. For an interesting presentation, serve these as a bed for roasted salmon or tuna and top with a delicate sauce. The potatoes complement the fish perfectly. If you can't find Yukon Gold potatoes, use russets.

2 lb. Yukon Gold potatoes (about 6)
1 cup milk
½ cup butter
salt to taste

¼ tsp. freshly ground pepper
1 medium bulb garlic, roasted (see
    page 15)
¼ cup chopped fresh chives

Carefully wash potatoes with a vegetable brush. Remove eyes, but do not peel, and cut into quarters. Place potatoes in a large pot and just cover with cold water. Cover pot and bring to a boil. Reduce heat and simmer for 20 minutes or until tender. Carefully drain potatoes. Return potatoes to empty pot and heat over low heat to dry, stirring or shaking continuously. Remove from heat and mash potatoes with a heavy potato masher. Slowly add milk and butter, mashing continuously. Add salt, pepper and roasted garlic pulp and mix thoroughly. Add chives and mix well. Transfer to serving plates or a warm ceramic bowl. Serve immediately.

SPICY ROASTED POTATOES

We prefer to prepare this dish with red-skinned potatoes, but you can substitute any baking potato. Serve this as a side dish with fish, chicken, beef or lamb.

2 lb. small red-skinned potatoes
¼ cup olive oil
1 tbs. chili powder
½ tsp. dried basil
½ tsp. dried oregano
salt and pepper to taste

Heat oven to 450°. Carefully wash potatoes with a vegetable brush. Remove eyes, but do not peel. If using small potatoes, cut in half. If using larger potatoes, cut into 1½-inch cubes. Place potatoes in a medium bowl and toss with oil, chili powder, basil, oregano, salt and pepper until well coated. Place potatoes in a single layer in a baking dish. Roast for 45 minutes, turning occasionally, until tender when pierced with a sharp knife. Serve warm.

ROASTED SWEET POTATO WEDGES

Servings: 2-3

Even folks who don't care for sweet potatoes give this recipe high praise. The curry adds a mild zing to the crusty potato wedges without overpowering the flavor. Serve these as a side dish with meat, poultry or seafood. You can also use russet potatoes.

1 lb. sweet potatoes
1½ tbs. olive oil
½ tsp. curry powder
¼ tsp. ground cumin
salt to taste

Heat oven to 375°. Peel sweet potatoes and cut in half. Cut each half into 6 wedges. In a large bowl, toss potato wedges with olive oil, curry, cumin and salt until well coated. Place potato wedges on a baking sheet and roast for about 30 minutes, turning occasionally, until tender when pierced with a sharp knife. Serve warm.

ROASTED SHRIMP AND VEGETABLE RISOTTO

Absolutely fabulous! In larger portions, this side dish can be served as a satisfying meal. The distinctive rich flavors and dramatic presentation of this dish make the physical effort of making it easily worthwhile. Be sure to serve it hot in individual ceramic bowls.

1 medium bulb fennel
¼ cup olive oil
½ lb. medium shrimp, peeled, deveined
½ cup sliced black olives
2 plum tomatoes, chopped
3 cups chicken stock
¼ cup finely chopped onion
2 tsp. minced shallots
1 clove garlic, minced or pressed
1 cup Arborio rice
¼ cup dry white wine
1 tsp. dried basil
¼ cup freshly grated Parmesan cheese

Heat oven to 450°. Cut fennel bulb into quarters, remove core, separate sections and cut each section into 1-inch pieces. In a medium bowl, toss fennel with 2 tbs. of the olive oil. Place fennel in a small roasting pan and roast for 15 to 18 minutes, stirring occasionally; remove from oven and set aside. Place shrimp, olives, and tomatoes in a small roasting pan and roast for 8 to 10 minutes until shrimp turn pink and are cooked through. Remove from oven and set aside.

Bring chicken stock to a boil, reduce heat and keep at a simmer. Heat remaining 2 tbs. olive oil in a large saucepan. Add onion, shallots and garlic and sauté over medium heat for 3 to 5 minutes, until onion is soft. Add rice and stir to coat grains with oil. Add wine and stir continuously until absorbed. Add ½ cup of the hot chicken stock to rice, stirring constantly until stock is absorbed. Repeat with remaining stock, ½ cup at a time. When rice is tender, but still slightly firm at the center, *al dente*, stir in fennel, shrimp, olives, tomatoes and basil, stirring constantly until mixed and heated through, about 2 minutes. You may not need to use all of the stock. Remove from heat and stir in Parmesan cheese. Serve immediately.

ROASTED MUSHROOM RISOTTO

Servings: 4

To retain its wonderful flavor, spoon the hot risotto into warm individual stoneware or ceramic bowls and serve immediately as an accompaniment to a main course of seafood, poultry or beef.

¼ cup olive oil
3 cloves garlic, minced or pressed
2 tbs. balsamic vinegar
½ tsp. dried basil
½ tsp. dried oregano
½ lb. shiitake mushrooms, stems removed, halved
½ lb. oyster mushrooms, trimmed, halved
¼ lb. portobello mushrooms, stems removed,
    cut into ½-inch slices
¼ tsp. salt
¼ tsp. freshly ground pepper
3 cups chicken stock
¼ cup finely chopped onion
1 cup Arborio rice
¼ cup dry white wine
¼ cup freshly grated Parmesan cheese

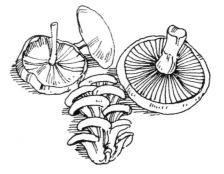

Heat oven to 450°. Combine 2 tbs. of the olive oil, 2 cloves of the minced garlic, balsamic vinegar, basil, oregano, mushrooms, salt and pepper in a medium bowl. Mix well until mushrooms are well coated. Place mushroom mixture in a medium-sized shallow roasting pan and roast for 20 minutes. Remove from oven and set aside.

Bring chicken stock to a boil, reduce heat and keep at a simmer. Heat remaining 2 tbs. olive oil in a large saucepan. Add onion and remaining minced garlic and sauté over medium heat for 3 to 5 minutes, until onion is soft. Add rice and stir to coat all grains with oil. Add wine and stir continuously until absorbed. Add ½ cup of the hot chicken stock to rice, stirring constantly until stock is absorbed. Repeat with remaining stock, ½ cup at a time. When rice is tender, but still slightly firm at the center, *al dente*, add mushroom mixture and stir until mixed and heated through, about 2 minutes. You may not need to use all of the stock. Remove from heat and stir in Parmesan cheese. Serve immediately.

ROASTED SOUTHWESTERN COUSCOUS

Servings: 6

What more could you possibly want? This dish tastes wonderful, looks beautiful, has wide appeal.

1 cup dry couscous
2¼ cups chicken stock
2 cloves garlic, minced or pressed
1 cup chopped red or green bell peppers
1 cup sliced fresh mushrooms
½ cup fresh or canned corn kernels
½ cup chopped carrots
¼ tsp. ground cumin
1 tsp. chili powder
salt and pepper to taste
2 tbs. olive oil
¼ cup chopped scallions

Heat oven 425°. Spread couscous on a baking sheet or ovenproof dish and roast for 5 to 6 minutes, until golden brown. Remove from oven and pour into a large bowl.

In a small saucepan, bring chicken stock to a boil. Pour stock over couscous and set aside until all liquid is absorbed, about 10 to 11 minutes. In a large bowl, combine garlic, peppers, mushrooms, corn, carrots, cumin, chili powder, salt, pepper and olive oil and mix well. Spread vegetable mixture on a baking sheet or ovenproof dish and roast for 13 to 15 minutes. Remove from oven, add to couscous and mix well. Stir in scallions. Fluff couscous with a fork before serving.

BROWN RICE WITH VEGETABLES AND ROASTED CHESTNUTS

Servings: 4

Here's a low-fat dish that's hearty and satisfying. If fresh chestnuts are out of season, you can substitute the bottled variety, which can be found in some grocery stores and in most specialty food stores.

2 cups roasted, shelled, peeled
    chestnuts (see page 10)
1 tbs. canola oil
2 cloves garlic, minced or pressed
1 medium onion, diced
1 bulb fennel, finely chopped

1 medium red bell pepper, diced
1 cup fresh or frozen green peas
1½ cups chicken stock
¾ cup brown rice
¼ tsp. freshly ground pepper
salt to taste

Grate chestnuts with a box grater and set aside. In a deep, straight-sided sauté pan, heat oil over medium-high heat. Add garlic, onion and fennel and sauté for 3 to 5 minutes, until onion is soft. Add diced peppers and peas and sauté for 2 minutes. Add chicken stock, rice, grated chestnuts, pepper and salt and stir well. Cover and bring to a boil. Reduce heat to low and simmer for 50 minutes or until liquid is absorbed, stirring occasionally. Serve warm.

FESTIVE ROASTED CHESTNUT STUFFING

This stuffing is a tantalizing blend of flavors, and is perfect for a winter holiday celebration. Stuff cooled stuffing loosely into the poultry cavity.

2 cups roasted, shelled, peeled chestnuts (see page 10)
1/4 cup butter
1/2 cup finely chopped onion
1/2 cup finely chopped celery
1 cup finely chopped mushrooms
4 cups day-old bread, cut into 1/2-inch cubes
1 tsp. dried thyme
1 tsp. dried sage
1/4 tsp. freshly ground pepper
salt to taste

Chop chestnuts into small pieces and set aside. Melt butter in a skillet over medium heat. Add onion and celery and sauté for about 4 minutes. Add mushrooms and sauté for 3 minutes. In a large bowl, combine all ingredients and mix well. Cool completely before stuffing into a poultry cavity.

CLASSIC APRICOT AND WILD RICE STUFFING

Servings: 6-8

Stuffing should be loosely packed in the poultry cavity so it cooks thoroughly while it expands. Generally, you can place ¾ cup of stuffing into the cavity for each pound of poultry. Place any extra stuffing in a covered ovenproof casserole and cook it along with the bird during the last 1½ hours. To prevent bacteria from growing, you should stuff your bird just before it's ready to be placed in a hot oven. This recipe can easily be adjusted for larger or smaller birds.

2 tbs. butter
1 small yellow onion, finely chopped
1 stalk celery, chopped
½ cup chopped mushrooms
salt and pepper to taste

¾ cup coarsely chopped dried apricots
¼ cup chopped walnuts
¼ tsp. paprika
4 cups cooked wild rice
1 cup chicken stock

Melt butter in a skillet over medium-low heat. Add onion, celery, mushrooms, salt and pepper and sauté for 3 minutes. Remove from heat. In a bowl, combine onion mixture, apricots, walnuts, paprika and wild rice and mix well. While mixing, slowly add stock until all liquid is absorbed. Cool completely before stuffing into a poultry cavity.

ROASTED ACORN SQUASH

Servings: 2

This tasty side dish goes especially well with pork and chicken — and it's loaded with vitamin A. For a unique variation, fill each roasted squash cavity with fresh raspberries, blueberries or cooked cranberries.

1 medium acorn squash
2 tbs. brown sugar, packed
2 tbs. butter
$\frac{1}{4}$ tsp. cinnamon
$\frac{1}{8}$ tsp. ground cloves
$\frac{1}{8}$ tsp. ground cardamom
salt to taste

Heat oven to 375°. Cut squash in half and remove seeds. Pierce insides of squash with a fork in several places. Place squash, cut-side up, in a medium-sized roasting pan. Fill each squash cavity with 1 tbs. of the brown sugar and 1 tbs. of the butter and sprinkle with spices and salt. Roast for about 50 minutes, until tender when pierced with a sharp knife.

ROASTED RATATOUILLE

Servings: 4

This recipe produces a brilliant display of colors. The flavors are not overpowering, and go beautifully with steamed white rice or pasta. You can also serve it hot or chilled as a meal for two.

½ cup olive oil
2 cloves garlic, coarsely minced
1 medium onion, sliced into rings,
　layers separated
1 medium eggplant, peeled, cut into
　1-inch cubes
1 medium red bell pepper, cut into
　½-inch strips
1 medium green bell pepper, cut into
　½-inch strips

2 small zucchini, cut into ¼-inch rounds
1 small yellow crookneck squash, cut
　into ¼-inch rounds
6 plum tomatoes, chopped
¼ tsp. red pepper flakes
1 tsp. chopped fresh basil
1 tsp. chopped fresh oregano
¼ tsp. freshly ground pepper
salt to taste
1 tbs. chopped fresh parsley for garnish

Heat oven to 425°. In a large bowl, combine all ingredients, except parsley, and mix thoroughly. Arrange vegetables in a large metal roasting pan or baking dish. Roast for 45 minutes, stirring occasionally, until vegetables are tender. Garnish with fresh parsley.

ROASTED FENNEL

Not to be confused with fennel seed, fresh fennel looks like celery, but has a distinctive licorice flavor. Although you can serve it raw, it's even tastier when roasted. Look for fennel in the produce section of your supermarket. It's sometimes called finocchio or anise.

2 bulbs fennel
1 tbs. butter
1 tsp. olive oil
2 cloves garlic, thinly sliced

1 small onion, finely chopped
1 cup chicken stock
$\frac{1}{8}$ tsp. salt
$\frac{1}{4}$ tsp. freshly ground pepper

Heat oven to 425°. Slice fennel bulbs in half lengthwise, leaving each half intact. Trim tops only and discard any discolored or tough outer layers. Melt butter and oil in a large ovenproof skillet over medium heat. Add garlic and onion and sauté for about 3 minutes, until soft. Remove garlic and onion from skillet and set aside. Place fennel cut-side down in skillet and cook for 6 to 7 minutes. Add chicken stock, salt, pepper and garlic-onion mixture and stir well. Cover, place skillet in oven and roast for 25 to 28 minutes until tender. Remove from oven and transfer to warm individual serving plates. Serve hot.

ROASTED ZUCCHINI, SUN-DRIED TOMATOES AND PROSCIUTTO

Servings: 2

Roasted zucchini lovers will applaud when they sample the delightful flavors of this recipe. Serve this dish beside fresh pasta topped with your favorite tomato sauce and hot crusty garlic bread. For a variation, you can substitute yellow crookneck squash in place of the zucchini.

1/2 cup dry sun-dried tomatoes
1 tbs. extra virgin olive oil
2 medium zucchini, halved lengthwise
2 cloves garlic, minced or pressed
6 slices prosciutto, cut into 3-inch pieces

1/4 tsp. dried thyme, or 1 tsp. fresh leaves
1/8 tsp. freshly ground pepper
1/4 cup freshly grated Parmesan cheese

Heat oven to 400°. Rehydrate sun-dried tomatoes in boiling water for 3 to 4 minutes, or according to package directions. Chop tomatoes. Coat a medium roasting pan with 1/2 tbs. of the olive oil. Place zucchini halves skin-side down in pan and sprinkle with minced garlic. Place prosciutto pieces over garlic and sprinkle with chopped sun-dried tomatoes, thyme and pepper. Drizzle with remaining olive oil and roast for 25 minutes, until tender. Remove from oven and sprinkle with Parmesan cheese. Serve immediately.

80 SIDE DISHES

ROASTED HONEY-MAPLE CARROTS

Servings: 3-4

Since fresh carrots are always available, you can serve this dish any time of the year. It's a colorful and flavorful dish that goes well with fish or poultry.

4-5 carrots
1 tsp. honey
1 tsp. maple syrup
⅛ tsp. ground cloves
salt to taste

Heat oven to 425°. Cut carrots into thin slices, about 4 inches long. In a medium bowl, toss carrots slices with honey, maple syrup, ground cloves and salt until well coated. Lightly coat a small roasting pan with nonstick cooking spray and add carrots. Roast for 10 to 12 minutes, until carrots are tender.

ROASTED GREEN BEANS

Crunchy and full of flavor, roasted green beans can be served with just about any dish.

1 lb. fresh green beans
3 tbs. extra virgin olive oil
juice from $\frac{1}{2}$ lemon
$\frac{3}{4}$ tsp. garlic powder
$\frac{1}{4}$ tsp. dried basil
salt and freshly ground pepper to taste

Heat oven to 500°. Snip tips from both ends of beans. Place beans on a baking sheet in a single layer. You may need to use 2 baking sheets. Drizzle with olive oil and roast for 7 to 8 minutes or until tender, turning occasionally. Remove from oven and transfer to a large serving bowl. Toss with fresh lemon juice, garlic powder, basil, salt and freshly ground pepper. Mix thoroughly and serve warm or at room temperature.

ROASTED CHESTNUT AND APPLE SAUTÉ

This tasty and satisfying side dish goes especially well with lamb or pork. If fresh chestnuts are out of season, you can substitute the bottled variety that can be found in some grocery stores and most specialty food stores. Use Cortland, Baldwin or Granny Smith apples.

1 cup roasted, shelled, peeled chestnuts (see page 10)
1 large apple
1 tbs. butter
1 tbs. canola or olive oil
1 medium-sized yellow onion, diced
¼ cup maple syrup
1 tbs. finely chopped walnuts

Chop roasted chestnuts coarsely. Peel and core apple and cut into wedges. In a skillet, melt butter with oil over medium heat. Add onion and sauté for 4 to 5 minutes. Add apple wedges and chestnuts and sauté for 6 to 8 minutes. Reduce heat to low and stir in maple syrup and walnuts. Serve warm.

POULTRY

BARBECUE ROASTED CHICKEN

The tangy barbecue sauce adds a wonderful zest and prevents the chicken from drying out.

1 tbs. butter
1½ tbs. finely chopped onion
1½ tsp. Worcestershire sauce
½ cup ketchup
¾ tsp. soy sauce

¼ tsp. dry mustard
¾ tsp. brown sugar
2¼ tsp. cider vinegar
6-8 chicken legs, thighs, or breast
    halves with skin

Melt butter in a skillet over medium heat. Add onion and sauté for 2 to 3 minutes. Add all remaining ingredients except chicken. Bring to a boil, reduce heat to a simmer and cook for 20 minutes, stirring occasionally. Cool completely. Rinse chicken and pat dry. Combine chicken and ¾ of the sauce in a shallow ovenproof casserole and marinate in the refrigerator for 2 hours.

Heat oven to 450°. Roast chicken for 30 to 33 minutes, until juices run clear when thickest piece of chicken is pierced with a knife. Baste occasionally with remaining sauce. Serve warm.

ROASTED CHICKEN CACCIATORE

Here's a simple-to-prepare, low-fat dish that delivers big flavor. Serve it with a tossed green salad and hot rolls.

4 chicken breast halves
1 medium onion, chopped
2 cloves garlic, coarsely minced
2 cups sliced mushrooms
1 medium red bell pepper, diced
1 medium green bell pepper, diced
½ cup chicken stock
2 cups diced fresh tomatoes
¼ tsp. dried basil
¼ tsp. dried thyme
⅛ tsp. salt
¼ tsp. freshly ground pepper
Roasted Tomato Sauce, page 14
1 tbs. minced fresh parsley for garnish

Heat oven to 425°. Rinse chicken, pat dry and place in a medium roasting pan. Add onion, garlic, mushrooms, peppers and chicken stock to pan and roast for 15 minutes.

Reduce oven heat to 375°. Add tomatoes, basil, thyme, salt and pepper. Roast for 40 minutes, stirring occasionally. Heat *Roasted Tomato Sauce* in a saucepan over medium-low heat until heated through. Remove chicken from oven, top with warmed tomato sauce and sprinkle with fresh parsley.

ROASTED BALSAMIC DIJON CHICKEN

This recipe also works well with skinless, boneless breasts of chicken, but you need to reduce the roasting time to about 20 minutes. For a variation, substitute another type of mustard for Dijon. Serve it with steamed rice and fresh vegetables.

2½-3 lb. chicken parts, skin removed
¼ cup balsamic vinegar
2 tbs. Dijon mustard
1 tbs. minced shallots

1 tsp. dried thyme
½ tsp. dried rosemary
⅛ tsp. salt
¼ tsp. freshly ground pepper

Rinse chicken and pat dry. In a small bowl, combine vinegar, mustard, shallots, thyme, rosemary, salt and pepper and mix well. Combine chicken with vinegar mixture in a ceramic casserole just large enough to hold chicken and marinade. Carefully coat all sides of chicken with marinade. Cover and refrigerate for 2 hours, turning chicken occasionally.

Heat oven to 400°. Arrange chicken in a roasting pan, pour marinade over chicken and roast for about 40 minutes, until a thermometer reads 170° when inserted in breast, or until juices run clear when thickest part of breast is pierced with a knife. Baste chicken occasionally with marinade while roasting.

CITRUS ROASTED CHICKEN

A well-prepared chicken always makes an appealing presentation.

¼ cup orange juice
2 tbs. lime juice
1 tsp. grated fresh lime peel (zest)
1 tsp. red pepper flakes
3 tbs. *Roasted Garlic Oil*, page 16
2 tbs. soy sauce

¾ tsp. ground ginger
1 tbs. honey
1 roasting chicken, about 4-5 lb.
salt and pepper
½ lime
½ orange

Heat oven to 375°. In a small bowl, combine orange juice, lime juice, lime zest, pepper flakes, oil, soy sauce, ginger and honey and mix well. Remove giblets from chicken and discard. Rinse chicken and pat dry. Season chicken cavity with salt and pepper and insert ½ lime and ½ orange. Truss chicken loosely with chicken string (see page 3) and place breast-side up on a nonstick or liberally oiled roasting rack in a roasting pan. Baste chicken with citrus mixture and roast for 2¾ to 3½ hours, until a thermometer reads 170° when inserted in breast, or until juices run clear when thickest part of breast is pierced with a knife. Baste frequently with citrus mixture while roasting. Transfer chicken to a serving platter, cover loosely and let sit for 15 minutes before carving into serving pieces.

FAVORITE ROASTED CHICKEN

Servings: 2-4

An adjustable, nonstick, V-shaped roasting rack allows for good air circulation, easy releasing and uniform roasting. If you purchase a professional-quality rack, you can use it to hold heavier birds and other meats.

¼ cup butter, melted
1 tbs. fresh lemon juice
1 roasting chicken, about 4-5 lb.

salt and pepper
1 tbs. fresh thyme leaves, or 1 tsp. dried
½ lemon

Heat oven to 475°. Combine melted butter and lemon juice and set aside. Remove giblets from chicken and discard. Rinse chicken and pat dry. Season chicken cavity with salt and pepper and sprinkle with thyme. Insert ½ lemon into cavity and truss chicken loosely with kitchen string (see page 3). Place chicken breast-side down on a nonstick or liberally oiled roasting rack in a roasting pan. Roast for 30 minutes, basting every 10 to 15 minutes with melted butter mixture. Reduce oven heat to 325°. Turn chicken breast-side up and roast for 30 to 45 minutes, basting every 10 to 15 minutes with butter mixture and pan juices, until a thermometer reads 170° when inserted in breast, or until juices run clear when thickest part of breast is pierced with a knife. Transfer chicken to a serving platter, breast-side up. Cover loosely and let sit for 15 minutes before carving into serving pieces.

VERTICALLY ROASTED GARLIC CHICKEN

Servings: 2-4

Vertical roasting racks are amazingly simple to use and roast a perfectly moist, delicious and healthy chicken every time without adding salt or fat, and without basting or turning.

1 roasting chicken, about 4-5 lb.
2 cloves garlic, thinly sliced
1 small onion, chopped
1 tsp. dried basil
1 tbs. fresh lemon juice

Heat oven to 400°. Remove giblets from chicken and discard. Rinse chicken and pat dry. Position chicken over rack, thread rack through chicken cavity, and press down until the top of rack comes through the neck area of chicken. Starting at the neck, carefully separate chicken skin from chicken meat down to the breast. Stuff garlic, onion and basil under skin. Drizzle chicken with lemon juice. Place chicken on rack in a roasting pan filled with ½ inch of water. Roast for about 1 hour, until a thermometer reads 170° when inserted in breast, or until juices run clear when thickest part of breast is pierced with a knife. Let chicken sit on rack, loosely covered, for 15 minutes before carving into serving pieces. For ease, carve chicken while still on rack.

ROASTED CORNISH GAME HENS WITH SAUSAGE STUFFING

You can substitute carrots for the parsnips in this moist and flavorful dish. Look for farmstand parsnips, picked during the cold winter months, for optimum sweet flavor. Unlike carrots, parsnips develop their sweetness as they age. Look for large ones. To reconstitute dried mushrooms, boil in a small amount of water for 5 minutes. Let sit for 30 minutes and drain well.

¼ lb. sweet Italian sausage
2 stalks celery, finely chopped
1 medium yellow onion, finely chopped
½ cup dried shiitake mushrooms,
    reconstituted, sliced
3 cups cooked wild rice
1 tbs. chopped fresh parsley
¼ tsp. dried basil
¼ tsp. dried thyme
¼ tsp. freshly ground pepper

1¾ cups chicken stock
4 rock Cornish game hens,
    1½-1¾ lb. each
2 tbs. olive oil
⅛ tsp. salt
¼ tsp. sweet paprika
2 medium yellow onions, cut into 8
    wedges
4 medium parsnips, cut into
    ½-inch rounds

Chop sausage into small pieces and sauté in a medium skillet over medium heat for 4 minutes. Drain fat and discard. Add celery, chopped onion and sliced, reconstituted mushrooms to skillet and sauté for 4 minutes. Cool completely.

Heat oven to 400°. In a large bowl, combine sausage mixture, rice, parsley, basil, thyme and 1/8 tsp. of the pepper and mix well. Add 3/4 cup of the chicken stock, mix well and set aside. Remove necks and giblets from hens and discard. Rinse hens and pat dry. Rub hens with olive oil and sprinkle cavities and exteriors with remaining pepper and salt. Sprinkle paprika on oiled exterior. Stuff hens with sausage mixture and place in a roasting pan large enough so that hens don't touch. Spread onion wedges and parsnips around hens. Add remaining chicken stock to pan and roast for 15 minutes. Reduce oven heat to 350° and roast for about 1 hour, until juices run clear when thigh is pierced with a knife. Baste occasionally with pan juices. Serve on warm individual serving plates.

ROASTED TURKEY BREAST
WITH WINTER VEGETABLES

Servings: 3-5

Slow roasting allows the vegetables and turkey to infuse with the spices for a low-fat meal you can't refuse.

1 tsp. dry mustard
1/2 tsp. sweet paprika
1/2 tsp. freshly ground pepper
1/2 tsp. dried thyme
1/2 tsp. dried basil
1/4 tsp. dried sage
1/4 tsp. dried rosemary
1/4 tsp. dried oregano
1 turkey breast, about 5 lb.
5 medium carrots, cut into 1/2-inch rounds
salt to taste
1/2 tsp. olive oil
12 medium red-skinned potatoes, cut into 1 1/2-inch chunks
1 medium yellow onion, cut into 8 wedges
2 1/2 cups low-sodium chicken stock

Heat oven to 375°. In a small bowl, combine brown mustard, paprika, ¼ tsp. of the ground pepper and thyme; mix well and set aside. In another small bowl, combine basil, sage, rosemary and oregano; mix well and set aside.

Rinse turkey breast and pat dry. Place sliced carrots in a nonstick roasting pan and sprinkle with basil mixture. Rub turkey with oil, remaining ¼ tsp. ground pepper and salt. Place turkey bone-side down in the center of pan on top of carrots. Surround turkey with potatoes and onion wedges. Distribute mustard mixture over turkey, potatoes and onions. Pour chicken stock into pan and roast for about 2 hours, until a thermometer reads 170° when inserted in breast, or until juices run clear when thickest part of breast is pierced with a knife. Transfer turkey and vegetables to a warm serving platter, cover loosely with foil or parchment paper and let sit until ready to serve. Pour pan drippings into a skillet, remove excess fat and discard. Heat pan juices on the stovetop over medium heat for about 5 minutes. Serve pan juices over individual portions of sliced turkey and vegetables.

LEMON-PEPPER ROASTED TURKEY BREAST

Servings: 3-4

This nourishing and inexpensive dish makes an ideal low-fat supper. It has wide appeal, making it a great choice to serve to guests. Serve with vegetables and rice.

1 tbs. fresh lemon juice
¼ tsp. freshly ground pepper
½ tsp. dried marjoram
¼ tsp. onion powder
⅛ tsp. salt

1 turkey breast, about 2½ lb.
3 stalks celery, cut into 2-inch strips
1 medium yellow onion, cut into 8
  wedges
1 cup water

Heat oven to 400°. In a small bowl, combine lemon juice, pepper, marjoram, onion powder and salt. Rinse turkey breast and pat dry. Loosen skin from breast by inserting your hand under skin and gently pressing on meat. Rub lemon-pepper mixture on breast meat under skin. Spray a roasting pan with nonstick cooking spray. Arrange celery and onion in roasting pan. Place turkey bone-side down in the center of pan on top of celery and onion; add water. Roast for about 1½ hours, until a thermometer reads 170° when inserted in breast, or until juices run clear when thickest part of breast is pierced with a knife. Transfer turkey to a warm serving platter, cover loosely with foil or parchment paper and let sit for 12 minutes. Slice turkey and serve with roasted vegetables.

IN A HURRY ROASTED TURKEY

Cooking at a high temperature produces a moist and flavorful roasted bird.

$\frac{1}{2}$ tsp. freshly ground pepper
$\frac{1}{2}$ tsp. salt
$\frac{1}{2}$ tbs. dried sage
$\frac{1}{2}$ tbs. dried rosemary, crushed
$\frac{1}{2}$ tbs. dried thyme

$\frac{1}{2}$ tbs. dried marjoram
1 turkey, about 10-12 lb.
1 clove garlic, thinly sliced
2 medium yellow onions, quartered

Heat oven to 475°. In a small bowl, combine pepper, salt, sage, rosemary, thyme and marjoram; mix well and set aside. Remove giblets from turkey and discard. Rinse turkey and pat dry. Loosen skin from turkey by inserting your hand under skin and pressing gently on meat, from the neck cavity down along the breast and drumsticks. Tuck garlic slices and rub $\frac{1}{2}$ of the herb mixture under skin. Sprinkle turkey cavity with remaining herb blend and insert onions. Truss turkey with kitchen string (see page 3). Place turkey breast-side up on a nonstick or liberally oiled V-shaped rack in a roasting pan. Roast for about $1\frac{1}{2}$ hours, until a thermometer reads 170° when inserted in breast, or until juices run clear when thickest part of breast is pierced with a knife. Transfer turkey to a warm serving platter, cover loosely with foil or parchment and let sit for 15 minutes before carving into serving pieces.

HOME FOR THE HOLIDAYS
ROASTED TURKEY WITH TURKEY GRAVY

The list of necessary kitchen equipment to produce a perfectly roasted turkey includes: a large metal roasting pan, a bulb baster, an instant-read meat thermometer, a pastry brush, a gravy separator, kitchen string and poultry skewers. For best results, purchase a fresh turkey from a reputable purveyor and never stuff your bird before you're ready to place it in the oven.

1 turkey, about 18-22 lb.
Classic Apricot and Wild Rice Stuffing,
    page 76
¼ cup butter, softened

salt and pepper
2 cups water
¼ cup butter, melted
Turkey Gravy, follows

Heat oven to 325°. Remove giblets from turkey and discard. Rinse turkey, pat dry and let turkey sit for 1 hour at room temperature. Spoon cooled stuffing loosely into turkey cavity. Secure skin over stuffed neck cavity with a poultry skewer. Use small skewers and string to secure large cavity and tie legs together loosely. Rub softened butter evenly over turkey skin and sprinkle with salt and pepper. Truss turkey with kitchen string (see page 3).

Place turkey breast-side up on a nonstick or liberally oiled roasting rack in a roasting pan and pour 2 cups water into pan. Roast turkey for 4½ to 5 hours, basting with butter and pan drippings every 25 minutes, until a thermometer reads 170° when inserted in breast, or until juices run clear when thickest part of breast is pierced with a knife. Transfer turkey to a large warm serving platter, cover loosely with foil or parchment paper and let sit for 15 minutes before carving into serving pieces. Serve with *Turkey Gravy*.

TURKEY GRAVY

pan juices from roasted turkey
up to 2 cups water or chicken stock

¼ cup flour
salt and pepper to taste

Pour pan drippings from roasting pan into a gravy separator or bowl. Separate fat from juices with separator, or skim fat from top of bowl with a ladle or large spoon; discard fat. Pour juices into a liquid measuring cup and add water or chicken stock to make 2¼ cups liquid. Place roasting pan on stovetop and pour all but ½ cup liquid into pan. Mix remaining ½ cup liquid with flour. Heat liquid in roasting pan to a boil, scrape up browned bits and pour into a saucepan. Heat over medium-high heat, slowly add flour mixture and stir continuously until mixture comes to a boil. Add salt and pepper and reduce to a simmer. Stir continuously for 8 to 10 minutes until thickened. Pour into a gravy boat and serve over turkey pieces.

MEATS

ROASTED SPARERIBS
WITH TANGY BARBECUE SAUCE

This is an ideal dish to serve at a casual party or on a buffet. It's full of sensational flavors and is visually appealing. For a variation, serve the barbecue sauce on chicken, turkey, sausage or sirloin steak.

1 cup ketchup
¼ cup Worcestershire sauce
2 tbs. balsamic vinegar
2 tbs. fresh lemon juice
4 tsp. fresh lime juice

¼ tsp. freshly ground pepper
1 tsp. dry mustard
1½-2 lb. pork spareribs, cut into
    individual pieces

In a medium bowl, combine all ingredients except spareribs and mix well. Place ribs in a shallow bowl, add sauce and toss to coat all ribs thoroughly. Cover and refrigerate for 4 hours or overnight.

Heat oven to 400°. Place ribs and ¾ of the barbecue sauce in a medium roasting pan and roast for 15 minutes. Reduce oven heat to 325° and roast ribs for about 1½ hours. Baste frequently with remaining sauce and turn occasionally. Serve warm.

ROASTED HAM WITH APRICOT SAUCE

Discerning palates will go wild over this crowd-pleasing dish that's ideal for a special feast or a celebration meal during the holidays.

1 fully cooked smoked country ham, bone in, about 10-14 lb.
whole cloves
2½ cups apple juice
1½ cups dry sherry
1 cup chopped dried apricots
1 cup apricot preserves
½ cup apricot brandy

Place ham in a large roasting pan, fat-side up. With a sharp knife, score fat in a diamond-shaped pattern. Insert a whole clove in the crossed points of each diamond. Pour apple juice and dry sherry over ham. In a medium bowl, combine dried apricots, apricot preserves and apricot brandy. Mix well and pour over ham. Cover and refrigerate for 5 to 6 hours.

Heat oven to 350°. Roast ham uncovered for 15 to 18 minutes per pound, basting occasionally with marinade, until a thermometer inserted in the center reads 140°. Remove ham from pan and let sit on a warm serving platter for 10 to 15 minutes before slicing into serving pieces.

With a slotted spoon, remove apricot pieces from roasting pan and set aside. Pour pan drippings into a gravy separator or bowl. Separate fat from juices with separator, or skim fat from top of bowl with a ladle or large spoon; discard fat. Heat juices in a medium saucepan over medium heat until bubbly; add apricot pieces and heat through. Slice ham and top with apricot sauce.

ROASTED PORK TENDERLOIN
WITH FRESH CRANBERRIES

This outstanding combination of luscious flavors comes together beautifully for a celebrated meal.

1 pork tenderloin, about 1-1½ lb., trimmed
1 large onion, quartered, layers separated
8-10 small red-skinned potatoes, quartered
1 cup fresh cranberries
1 tsp. olive oil
2 cloves garlic, minced or pressed
½ cup cranberry juice
½ cup orange juice
1 tsp. grated fresh orange peel (zest)
½ tsp. dry mustard
1 tbs. honey
1 tsp. dried thyme
salt to taste

Heat oven to 425°. Place tenderloin in a lightly greased large roasting pan. Scatter onion, potatoes and cranberries around pork. In a medium skillet, heat olive oil over medium-low heat and sauté garlic for 1 minute. Add cranberry juice, orange juice and orange zest. Bring to a boil and cook until reduced by $\frac{1}{2}$, about 5 minutes. Remove from heat and whisk in dry mustard, honey, thyme and salt. Pour over tenderloin and vegetables and roast for 10 minutes. Reduce oven heat to 325° and roast for 45 to 50 minutes, until a thermometer inserted in the center of pork reads 160° for medium and 170° for well done*. Remove pork from oven and transfer to a warm serving platter. Let sit for 10 minutes before slicing into serving pieces. Transfer potatoes, onion and cranberries to a serving bowl or scatter around sliced pork on serving platter.

*Some health authorities discourage eating undercooked meat because of possible bacterial contamination.

HERB-ENCRUSTED
ROASTED PORK TENDERLOIN

This goes very nicely with roasted potato wedges and fresh asparagus. It's also great with mashed potatoes and applesauce or a fruit chutney.

1 tsp. dried thyme
1 tsp. dried sage
1 tsp. cinnamon
2 tsp. ground cumin

¼ tsp. garlic powder
1 pork tenderloin, about 2-2½ lb.,
   trimmed
3 tbs. olive oil

Heat oven to 400°. In a small bowl, combine thyme, sage, cinnamon, cumin and garlic powder. Brush pork with olive oil and rub with herb mixture. Heat a large nonstick skillet over medium-high heat and brown pork on all sides. Place browned pork in a roasting pan and roast for about 30 minutes, until a thermometer inserted in the center of pork reads 160° for medium and 170° for well done*. Remove pork from oven, transfer to a serving platter and let sit for 10 minutes before slicing into serving pieces.

*Some health authorities discourage eating undercooked meat because of possible bacterial contamination.

ROASTED PORK CHOPS
WITH LIME AND GINGER

Servings: 2-4

This recipe works well in a portable electric or conventional oven. Portable electric roaster ovens are convenient and a nice supplement to your kitchen oven. The intense heat will sear the meat to create a deep, rich flavor. You can fit 4 chops comfortably in a 6-quart portable electric roaster oven. For large portable ovens, increase the quantity or place the chops in a baking dish.

1/4 cup low-sodium soy sauce
2 tbs. dry white wine
2 tbs. fresh lime juice
1/2 tbs. brown sugar, packed
2 shallots, minced

2 cloves garlic, minced or pressed
1 small onion, minced
1 tbs. ginger, minced
4 pork chops, 1 inch thick

In a medium bowl, combine all ingredients except pork chops and mix well. Place pork chops in a shallow baking dish and pour marinade over chops. Marinate, covered, in the refrigerator for 2 to 4 hours or overnight. Heat oven to 350°. Place chops and marinade in a shallow baking dish and roast for about 45 minutes, until a thermometer inserted in the center of pork reads 160° for medium and 170° for well done*.

*Some health authorities discourage eating undercooked meat because of possible bacterial contamination.

STUFFED PORK CHOPS WITH OVEN-ROASTED TOMATO-PEPPER SAUCE

Servings: 2

You can prepare this recipe in a conventional oven or a portable electric roaster oven for equally excellent results. Serve the sauce on top of pork, fish, poultry or beef or on the side as a dipping sauce. It yields about 3 cups.

SAUCE

8 plum tomatoes, peeled, seeded
1 tbs. olive oil
5 tbs. dry sherry
3/4 tsp. dried basil
1 1/2 tsp. dried parsley
1 tsp. chili powder

dash cayenne pepper
salt to taste
2 cloves garlic, minced or pressed
1 large red bell pepper, roasted (see page 8)

PORK CHOPS

4 pork loin chops, 1-1 1/4 inches thick
1 tbs. butter
2 cloves garlic, minced
1 small onion, finely chopped
1 medium green bell pepper, finely chopped

1 cup herb stuffing mix or cubed dry bread
1/3 cup water
1 tsp. dried thyme
1 tsp. dried parsley
salt and pepper to taste

For sauce, heat oven to 425°. Place tomatoes in a medium roasting pan and drizzle with olive oil and sherry. Cover and roast for 50 minutes. Remove from oven and cool for 10 to 15 minutes. With a heavy potato masher, mash tomatoes into small chunks. Add basil, parsley, chili powder, cayenne pepper, salt and garlic and mix well. Return tomatoes to oven and roast for 20 minutes. While tomatoes are roasting, chop roasted pepper into small pieces. Transfer tomatoes to a medium bowl and add peppers. Mix well.

For pork, heat oven to 375°. Cutting from the fat side of pork chops, slice a pocket in the center of each chop, almost to the bone; set aside. Melt butter in a medium skillet over medium heat and sauté garlic, onion and green pepper for 3 to 5 minutes, until soft. Stir in stuffing mix, water, thyme, parsley, salt and pepper and mix well. Stuff each pork chop with ¼ of the stuffing mixture and secure with wooden picks. Place chops on a roasting rack in a medium roasting pan and roast for about 40 minutes, until a thermometer inserted in the center of chops reads 160° for medium and 170° for well done*. Remove from oven and place on individual serving plates, topped with sauce.

*Some health authorities discourage eating undercooked meat because of possible bacterial contamination.

ROASTED FLANK STEAK WITH BALSAMIC ROASTED ONIONS

When properly prepared, flank steak can create an exceptionally tasty, satisfying and economical meal. The technique of cutting the steak in half through the middle, or "butterflying," works well here.

1 flank steak, about 2 lb.
¼ cup olive oil
¼ cup soy sauce
¼ cup dry sherry
2 cloves garlic, minced or pressed
½ tsp. dry mustard
½ tsp. dried thyme
¼ tsp. freshly ground pepper
2 cups sliced *Balsamic Roasted Onions*, page 12

Place steak on a large cutting board, trim membranes and fat and discard. Starting at the long end, cut steak in half horizontally, but don't cut all the way through. Open steak like a book as you cut until steak is in one flat piece. Pound steak with a meat mallet until it is about ¼-inch thick. In a small bowl, combine oil, soy sauce, sherry, garlic, dry mustard, thyme and pepper and mix well. Place steak in a large, shallow dish. Pour oil mixture over steak and marinate in the refrigerator for 4 hours or overnight.

Heat oven to 350°. Remove steak from marinade, pat dry and lay flat. Spread onions lengthwise down one side of steak. Starting at the long end, roll steak tightly and tie with kitchen string in several places. Place stuffed steak in a lightly greased medium roasting pan and roast for 40 to 55 minutes, basting occasionally with marinade, until a thermometer inserted in the center of meat reads 155° for medium and 170° for well done*. Cool slightly and cut into 1-inch-thick slices.

*Some health authorities discourage eating undercooked meat because of possible bacterial contamination.

POT ROAST WITH FRESH VEGETABLES

Servings: 6

You will maximize the flavor and tenderness of these cuts of beef with a long, low-temperature cooking process. Although this dish isn't exactly roasted, in the strictest sense of the word, you'll love the comforting flavors and convenience of this one-pot meal.

2 tbs. olive oil
1 beef eye round or bottom round roast, about 3 lb.
1½ cups beef stock
½ cup dry sherry
2 bay leaves
¾ tsp. dried thyme
salt and pepper to taste
3 carrots, cut into 4-inch pieces
8 small red-skinned potatoes
2 celery stalks, cut into 2-inch pieces
1 large red onion, quartered, layers separated
4-6 small beets, peeled, quartered
1 can (14.5 oz.) stewed tomatoes with juice
4 cloves garlic

Heat oven to 250°. Heat oil in a large Dutch oven over medium-high heat on the stovetop. Add beef and brown all sides. Remove fat from pan and discard. Add beef stock, sherry, bay leaves, thyme, salt and pepper. Place in oven and roast for about 60 minutes, until a thermometer inserted in the center of meat reads 110°. Add all remaining ingredients. Increase oven heat to 500° and roast for about 30 to 40 minutes, until a thermometer inserted in the center of meat reads 140° for rare and 160° for medium*. Remove beef from pan and let stand for 10 to 15 minutes. Slice roast and place slices on a warm serving platter. Place vegetables around beef or in a separate warm serving bowl.

*Some health authorities discourage eating undercooked meat because of possible bacterial contamination.

STANDING RIB ROAST WITH PAN JUICES

Servings: 6-8

The long cooking process produces a tender and juicy roast. Follow the roasting times as a guide, but be sure to use a meat thermometer to get an accurate reading. Serve with **Roasted Garlic Mashed Potatoes**, *page 65.*

1 beef rib roast, about 4-6 lb.
4 carrots, unpeeled, cut into thirds
3 celery stalks with leaves, cut into thirds
1 medium red bell pepper, seeded, quartered
1 medium onion, unpeeled, quartered
8 cloves garlic, unpeeled
1½ cups beef stock
½ cup dry red wine
salt and pepper to taste

Heat oven to 325°. Place beef fat-side up in a large roasting pan. Scatter carrots, celery, pepper, onion and garlic around beef. Roast for 2 to 3¾ hours until a thermometer inserted in the center reads 135° for rare, 155° for medium and 170° for well done*. Remove roast from oven and place on a warm serving platter. Let sit for 15 minutes before slicing.

Remove excess fat from pan and discard. Add stock and wine to roasting pan with pan juices and vegetables. Place pan on the stovetop and bring to a boil. Cook, stirring, until liquid is reduced by 1/2. Strain mixture through a colander or mesh strainer, using the back of a large spoon to press juice from vegetables. Discard vegetables. Add salt and pepper.

To carve roast, insert a fork between the top 2 ribs. Slice from the fat side across to the bone. Cut down along the bone to loosen each slice of beef. Pour pan juices over sliced beef.

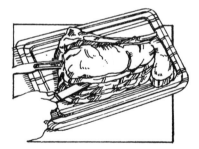

*Some health authorities discourage eating undercooked meat because of possible bacterial contamination.

OVEN-ROASTED SWISS STEAK WITH VEGETABLES

This recipe uses an economical, flavorful cut of beef.

3 tbs. all-purpose flour
½ tsp. dried basil
½ tsp. dried oregano
½ tsp. salt
½ tsp. freshly ground pepper
1 tip or chuck steak, about ¾-inch thick, 1½ lb.
3 tbs. olive oil

1 can (13 oz.) stewed tomatoes with juice
1 cup tomato sauce
1 clove garlic, minced or pressed
1 large onion, sliced
1 large green bell pepper, seeded, cut into ¼-inch strips
2 stalks celery, chopped

Heat oven to 350°. In a small bowl, combine flour, basil, oregano, salt and pepper and mix well. Sprinkle ½ of the flour mixture on one side of beef. Pound meat with a meat mallet until flour is absorbed. Turn beef over and repeat with remaining flour mixture. Heat oil in a large ovenproof skillet. Add beef and brown on all sides. Add remaining ingredients, place skillet in the oven and roast for about 1¾ hours, until a thermometer inserted in the center reads 155° for medium and 170° for well done*.

*Some health authorities discourage eating undercooked meat because of possible bacterial contamination.

ROASTED LEG OF LAMB WITH PAN GRAVY

Servings: 6-7

Garlic and rosemary enhance the tender, soft texture of lamb beautifully.

1 leg of lamb, hip bone removed, about
   6-7 lb., fat trimmed to $\frac{1}{8}$ inch
3 cloves garlic, thinly sliced
1 tbs. olive oil
1 tsp. dried rosemary, crushed
$\frac{1}{8}$ tsp. salt

$\frac{1}{2}$ tsp. freshly ground pepper
1 medium yellow onion, quartered,
   layers separated
1 cup low-sodium chicken stock
1 tbs. cornstarch

Heat oven to 400°. Pierce $\frac{1}{2}$-inch slits into lamb and insert garlic. Rub with oil and sprinkle with rosemary, salt and pepper. Place lamb in a shallow roasting pan, fat-side up, and arrange onion around lamb. Roast for about $1\frac{1}{2}$ hours, basting occasionally with pan drippings, until a thermometer inserted in the center reads 140° for rare, 160° for medium or 170° for well done*. Remove lamb from pan and let sit on a warm serving platter for 15 minutes before slicing into serving pieces. Remove fat from roasting pan and discard. Mix stock with cornstarch, add to pan juices and heat on the stovetop over medium-high heat. Stir continuously, scraping up browned bits, until thickened. Pour into a gravy boat and serve with sliced lamb.

*Some health authorities discourage eating undercooked meat because of possible bacterial contamination.

CROWN ROAST OF LAMB WITH SHIITAKE AND MINT STUFFING

Servings: 6-8

Surround the roast with assorted cooked seasoned vegetables, such as Brussels sprouts, carrots and/or roasted potatoes. Have your butcher prepare a crown roast made from 2 "Frenched" racks of lamb tied back-to-back. Parchment paper frills can be found at kitchenware and department stores.

STUFFING

2½ cups chicken stock
½ tsp. salt
1½ cups wild rice, rinsed, sorted, drained
1 tbs. butter
¼ cup chopped shallots

½ cup chopped shiitake mushrooms
¼ cup minced celery
1 tbs. finely chopped fresh mint
1 tbs. fresh thyme leaves
¼ tsp. freshly ground pepper

LAMB

1 crown roast lamb, 16 ribs
1½-2 tbs. olive oil
⅛ tsp. dried rosemary
⅛ tsp. dried thyme
⅛ tsp. dried basil

⅛ tsp. dried marjoram
1 clove garlic, minced or pressed
salt and pepper to taste
16 parchment paper frills, optional

For stuffing, bring chicken stock and salt to a boil in a medium saucepan. Add wild rice and cover pan. Reduce heat to low and simmer for 45 to 50 minutes, until all liquid is absorbed. In a medium skillet, heat butter over medium-high heat. Add shallots, mushrooms and celery and sauté for 3 minutes. Combine cooked wild rice with mushroom mixture, mint, thyme and pepper. Mix well and cool slightly.

For lamb, heat oven to 350°. Place 2 layers of parchment paper, 2 inches wider than crown roast, in a roasting pan. Place lamb, bones up, on parchment. Combine olive oil, rosemary, thyme, basil, marjoram and garlic, mix well and brush liberally over meat. Season meat with salt and pepper. Fill the center of roast with stuffing. Wrap foil onto the ends of each bone. Roast for about 1½ hours, until a thermometer inserted in the center of meat reads 140° for rare, 160° for medium or 170° for well done*. Remove from oven, cover with foil and let sit for 10 minutes. Transfer roast to a warm serving platter, supporting parchment paper on bottom to hold stuffing in place. Carefully slide parchment from under roast. Remove foil from bones. Place a parchment paper frill over each bone if desired. Slice lamb into chops and serve on individual plates with stuffing.

*Some health authorities discourage eating undercooked meat because of possible bacterial contamination.

ROASTED RACK OF LAMB

Servings: 6-8

To simplify preparation, ask your butcher to "French" the lamb racks, which refers to cleaning the ends of the racks so that the bones are exposed. This recipe can be easily halved. Serve with roasted potatoes and carrots.

2 racks lamb, trimmed, 8 chops per rack
2 tbs. extra virgin olive oil
1 clove garlic, halved
1/2 tsp. dried rosemary, crushed
1/4 tsp. freshly ground pepper
1/8 tsp. salt
4 fresh rosemary sprigs for garnish, optional
lemon wedges for garnish, optional

Cut each rack in half so that it has 4 ribs. Brush lamb with oil and rub with garlic. Sprinkle with rosemary, pepper and salt. Cover and refrigerate for 8 hours.

Heat oven to 400°. Heat a heavy roasting pan on the stovetop over medium-high heat and brown lamb on all sides. Place pan in oven and roast for 25 to 40 minutes, until a thermometer inserted in the center of meat reads 140° for rare, 160° for medium and 170° for well done*. Remove lamb from oven, cover loosely and let stand for 10 minutes. Slice lamb into chops and serve immediately on warm individual serving plates. Garnish with rosemary sprigs and/or lemon wedges if desired.

*Some health authorities discourage eating undercooked meat because of possible bacterial contamination.

FISH AND SHELLFISH

ROASTED SALMON FILLETS

Servings: 2-3

*Salmon is an excellent source of omega-3 fatty acids, which have known health benefits. We recommend using Alaskan salmon, which is a wild fish from clean waters. Salmon retains its firm texture and the flavor is greatly enhanced when roasted. For a memorable meal, serve this recipe with **Roasted Garlic Mashed Potatoes**, page 65, and a fresh garden salad.*

2 salmon fillets, about 1 lb.
2 tbs. olive oil
$\frac{1}{2}$ tsp. cracked black peppercorns

salt to taste
two $\frac{1}{4}$-inch-thick lemon slices for garnish
two 3-inch sprigs fresh dill for garnish

Heat oven to 400°. Rinse fish and pat dry. Heat oil in an ovenproof skillet or heavy metal roasting pan over medium-high heat. Place salmon skin-side up in pan and cook for about 5 seconds. Turn over, quickly sprinkle cracked peppercorns and salt over fish and place pan in oven. Roast for 10 to 13 minutes, depending on thickness, until the centers of fillets are opaque. Transfer salmon to warm serving plates. Garnish with lemon slices and dill sprigs. Serve immediately.

NOTE: To create a decorative garnish, make a slit in each lemon slice from the edge to the center. Twist the ends apart and insert a sprig of dill in the center. Place lemon slice with dill sprigs in the center of each roasted fillet.

OVEN-ROASTED SALMON
WITH A SWEET AND SPICY CRUST

A mildly spicy, sweet crust complements the distinctive flavor of the salmon perfectly. This very special dish is ideal to serve at a formal dinner party.

2 salmon fillets, about 1 lb.
2 tbs. molasses
3 tbs. brown sugar, packed
1/4 tsp. cayenne pepper
1 tsp. chili powder

1/4 tsp. ground cumin
1/4 tsp. freshly ground black pepper
1/2 tsp. water
2 dashes Tabasco Sauce
2 sprigs fresh cilantro for garnish

Heat oven to 400°. Rinse fish and pat dry. In a small bowl, combine molasses, brown sugar, cayenne, chili powder, cumin, pepper, water and Tabasco; mix well. Place salmon skin-side down in a lightly greased medium roasting pan. Spread equal amounts of molasses mixture over each fillet. Roast for 10 to 13 minutes, depending on thickness, until the centers of fillets are opaque. Transfer salmon to warm serving plates and garnish with fresh cilantro.

ZESTY ROASTED TUNA STEAKS

Servings: 2

Serve this spicy, picture-pretty dish with steamed summer squash and rice pilaf. This recipe also works beautifully with swordfish and halibut. Scotch bonnet and habanero chiles are very similar, and are among the hottest chile peppers available. If you desire a less fiery dish, use ¼ to ½ of the chile, or substitute a milder chile such as a serrano or jalapeño.

1 Scotch bonnet or habanero chile, seeded, finely chopped
2 scallions, finely chopped
3 tbs. fresh lemon juice
1 tsp. fresh lime juice
¼ tsp. freshly ground pepper
½ tsp. chili powder
⅛ tsp. ground cumin

¼ tsp. dried lemon peel
⅛ tsp. ground cloves
⅛ tsp. ground cinnamon
3 cloves garlic, minced or pressed
¼ tsp. freshly ground pepper
1 tbs. fresh lemon juice
½ tsp. olive oil
2 tuna steaks, about 1 lb.

In a small bowl, combine chile, scallions, lemon and lime juice and pepper. Mix well and refrigerate for several hours.

Heat oven to 375°. In a small bowl, combine chili powder, ground cumin, dried lemon peel, ground cloves, cinnamon, garlic, pepper, lemon juice and olive oil to form a thick paste. Rinse tuna steaks and pat dry. Place tuna in a lightly greased, medium roasting pan. Spread paste over the tops and sides of each tuna steak. Roast for about 20 minutes, until the centers of steaks are opaque. Transfer to warm serving plates and top with equal portions of chile and scallion mixture.

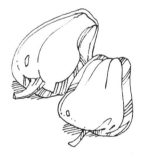

CURRY ROASTED SWORDFISH

Servings: 2-3

*Curry powder, a blend of spices, herbs and chiles, adds a pleasing spicy taste of to this dish. It's excellent paired with **Roasted Sweet Potato Wedges**, page 67, and a fresh garden salad.*

1/4 cup mayonnaise
1 clove garlic, minced or pressed
1 1/2 tsp. curry powder
1/2 tsp. chopped fresh parsley
salt to taste
2 swordfish steaks, about 1 lb.

Heat oven to 375°. In a small bowl, combine mayonnaise, garlic, curry powder, parsley and salt; mix well. Rinse fish and pat dry. Coat each steak with mayonnaise mixture. Place swordfish in a lightly greased roasting pan or baking dish and roast for about 20 minutes, until centers of steaks are just opaque. Heat broiler and broil fish until top is golden brown, about 2 to 3 minutes.

ROASTED SWORDFISH WITH GARLIC AND FENNEL SAUCE

This tasty recipe works just as well with tuna, halibut, salmon and striped bass. You'll notice a mild licorice flavor from the ground fennel. If you can't find ground fennel, you can easily grind whole fennel seeds with a mortar and pestle or electric spice grinder.

¼ cup olive oil
4 cloves garlic, thinly sliced
¼ cup fresh lemon juice
¼ tsp. ground fennel seeds

salt to taste
2 swordfish steaks, about 1 lb.
fresh parsley sprigs for garnish

Heat oven to 350°. Heat 3 tbs. of the olive oil in a small skillet over medium heat. Add garlic, lemon juice, ground fennel and salt and sauté for 2 to 3 minutes. Remove from heat and set aside. Rinse fish and pat dry. Lightly oil a medium roasting pan with remaining 1 tbs. olive oil and place fish in pan. Top fish with garlic and fennel sauce and roast for about 15 minutes, until centers of fish are just opaque. Heat broiler and broil fish until top is golden brown, about 2 to 3 minutes. Transfer to warm serving plates and garnish with fresh parsley sprigs.

ROASTED SANTA FE-STYLE SWORDFISH

Servings: 2

You can substitute tuna, shark, marlin or salmon in place of the swordfish — just be sure the fish is fresh. Perfect for today's busy lifestyle, you can prepare this attractive dish 6 to 8 hours in advance of roasting it, as long as you keep it covered and refrigerated. This dish goes particularly well with rice and steamed vegetables.

two 1-inch-thick swordfish steaks,
  about 1 lb.
1/3 cup fresh lime juice
2 tbs. minced fresh cilantro
2 tbs. minced red bell pepper

2 tbs. minced yellow bell pepper
1 tbs. minced scallions
1 tbs. minced jalapeño pepper
2 tbs. extra virgin olive oil
salt and freshly ground pepper to taste

Heat oven to 375°. Rinse fish and pat dry. Cut fish into 1½-inch cubes and combine with all other ingredients in a bowl. Mix thoroughly. Place swordfish mixture in a single layer in a medium roasting pan, or divide evenly between 2 individual ovenproof casseroles. Roast for about 20 minutes, until centers of steaks are opaque.

GROUPER ROASTED WITH LEMONS AND HERBS

This recipe works well with haddock, cod, snapper, scrod, pollack, hake, flounder and halibut — just about any mild fish will work.

3 lemons, halved
2 grouper fillets, about 1 lb.
2 tbs. olive oil
1/8 tsp. freshly ground pepper
salt to taste

1/4 tsp. dried basil
1/4 tsp. dried thyme
1 clove garlic, minced or pressed
4 sprigs fresh parsley for garnish
4 lemon wedges for garnish

Heat oven to 400°. Place lemon halves cut-side up in an ovenproof glass, ceramic or porcelain dish. Roast lemons for 20 minutes, cool for 5 minutes and squeeze juice into a small bowl. Rinse fish, pat dry and place in an ovenproof dish. Combine lemon juice with oil, pepper, salt, basil, thyme and garlic and pour over fish. Place fish uncovered in the coldest part of the refrigerator for 1 hour.

Heat oven to 400°. Remove and discard all marinade except 2 tbs. Roast fish with marinade for 10 to 15 minutes, until centers of fillets are opaque. Transfer fish to warm serving plates and garnish with parsley sprigs and lemon wedges.

BLACKENED ROASTED HALIBUT WITH TRICOLOR PEPPERS

This dish is easy to prepare and a joy to serve. The spicy, interesting dish is presented over a vibrant bed of slightly crisp vegetables.

BLACKENING SPICES

1 tbs. paprika
1 tbs. onion powder
1 tbs. garlic powder
1 tbs. black pepper
2 tsp. dried thyme

1 tsp. dried oregano
$\frac{1}{2}$ tsp. cayenne pepper
1 tsp. chili powder
$\frac{1}{4}$ tsp. salt

FISH

$\frac{1}{2}$ medium red bell pepper, cut into
$\quad$ $\frac{1}{4}$-inch strips
$\frac{1}{2}$ medium yellow bell pepper, cut into
$\quad$ $\frac{1}{4}$-inch strips
$\frac{1}{2}$ medium green bell pepper, cut into
$\quad$ $\frac{1}{4}$-inch strips
1 medium red onion, cut into
$\quad$ $\frac{1}{4}$-inch strips

$\frac{1}{4}$ cup olive oil
2 halibut steaks, about 1 lb.
2 tbs. butter, melted
lemon wedges for garnish
fresh cilantro or dill sprigs for garnish

130   FISH AND SHELLFISH

For blackening spices, combine all ingredients in a small bowl and store in an airtight container. Keep in a dark area, such as a drawer or kitchen cabinet, and use sparingly.

For fish, heat oven to 450°. Place pepper and onion strips in a medium roasting pan and toss with olive oil. Rinse fish and pat dry. Brush fish with melted butter. Pour 3 to 4 tbs. blackening spice mixture onto a sheet of waxed paper or into a shallow bowl. Dredge fish in mixture, covering both sides. Place coated fish on top of peppers and onions and roast for 8 minutes. Reduce oven heat to 350° and roast for about 10 minutes, until centers of steaks are opaque. Garnish with lemon wedges and fresh cilantro or dill sprigs.

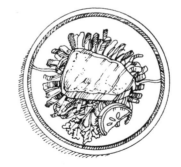

ROASTED GARLIC RED SNAPPER

Servings: 2

The secret ingredient in this recipe is the roasted garlic oil. It adds a pleasant, nutty, mild garlic flavor without overpowering the sweetness of the red snapper. Making your own roasted garlic oil is easy and economical. You can also purchase it at specialty food shops and some supermarkets. Try it with other seafood, vegetable or pasta dishes.

2 tbs. *Roasted Garlic Oil*, page 16
¼ cup dry white wine
2 tbs. fresh lemon juice
1 tsp. dried marjoram
¼ tsp. dried basil

⅛ tsp. freshly ground pepper
pinch salt
2 large red snapper fillets, about 1 lb.
lemon wedges for garnish
cilantro sprigs for garnish

In a small bowl, combine *Roasted Garlic Oil*, white wine, lemon juice, marjoram, basil, pepper and salt and mix well. Rinse fish and pat dry. Place fish in a shallow ceramic or glass dish. Pour marinade over fish and turn to coat all sides. Cover and refrigerate for 2 hours.

Heat oven to 400°. Place fish with marinade in a nonstick roasting pan. Roast fish uncovered for 5 minutes. Reduce oven heat to 350°, turn fish over, cover and roast for 10 minutes, until the centers of fillets are just opaque. Garnish with lemon wedges and cilantro sprigs.

RASPBERRY ROASTED HADDOCK

Servings: 3-4

The soft texture and mild flavor of haddock pairs beautifully with the delicate sweetness of fresh raspberries. This is a beautiful summer dish to serve, especially when the fragile raspberries are at their peak. You can substitute flounder, cod, scrod or pollack for haddock.

2 tbs. raspberry vinegar
1/2 tbs. grated fresh orange peel (zest)
1/2 cup olive oil
1/2 tsp. dried thyme
1 tbs. red raspberry preserves
1 clove garlic, minced or pressed

1/4 tsp. freshly ground pepper
salt to taste
2 haddock fillets, about 1 1/4-1 1/2 lb.
3/4 cup fresh raspberries
4 fresh mint leaves for garnish

In a medium bowl, whisk together raspberry vinegar, orange zest, olive oil, thyme, raspberry preserves, garlic, pepper and salt. Rinse fish and pat dry. Lightly coat a medium roasting pan with nonstick cooking spray and add fish. Pour preserves mixture over fish, cover and refrigerate for 3 to 4 hours.

Heat oven to 400°. Roast fish for 15 minutes. Top with 1/2 cup of the fresh raspberries and roast for about 5 minutes, until the centers of fillets are opaque, basting occasionally with marinade. Transfer fish to a warm serving plate, top with remaining fresh raspberries and garnish with mint leaves.

SHRIMP WITH ROASTED TOMATO SAUCE

Servings: 4

This intriguing, robust dish will remind you of your favorite Italian restaurant. It makes an impressive presentation that's ideal for a casual dinner party. Most of the preparation can be done in advance so you can spend time with your guests. Serve it over cooked angel hair pasta with fresh garlic bread and a garden salad.

1 lb. large shrimp, peeled, deveined
5 tbs. olive oil
2 cloves garlic, minced

1 medium onion, minced
4 cups *Roasted Tomato Sauce*, page 14
1 bay leaf

Rinse shrimp under cold running water and pat dry; refrigerate. In a medium sauté pan, heat 1 tbs. of the olive oil over medium heat. Add garlic and sauté for 2 minutes. Add onion and sauté for 3 to 5 minutes, until soft. Add *Roasted Tomato Sauce* and bay leaf and stir well. Bring to a boil, reduce heat, cover and simmer for 35 to 40 minutes.

Heat oven to 450°. Place shrimp in a roasting pan, taking care not to overlap. Drizzle with remaining 1/4 cup olive oil and roast for about 5 minutes, until just cooked through. Remove shrimp and discard oil. Add shrimp to sauce and heat through. Discard bay leaf.

ROASTED SHRIMP WITH FRESH TOMATOES

Servings: 4

We like to serve this dish with pasta tossed with a fruity extra virgin olive oil, chopped fresh basil and parsley, accompanied by a fresh mixed green salad. This meal is bursting with a blend of brilliant colors and mouthwatering aromas.

1 lb. large shrimp, unpeeled, legs removed
6 large vine-ripened tomatoes
2 cloves garlic, minced or pressed
1 tbs. minced fresh basil, or 1 tsp. dried
1 tsp. minced fresh oregano, or $\frac{1}{2}$ tsp. dried
2 tbs. dry white wine
salt and pepper to taste

Heat oven to 350°. Rinse shrimp and dry thoroughly. Place shrimp in a medium roasting pan, taking care not to overlap. Cut each tomato into 8 wedges and scatter tomato wedges over shrimp. Sprinkle minced garlic, basil, oregano, white wine, salt and pepper over tomatoes and shrimp. Roast for 18 minutes, until shrimp are cooked through. Transfer to warm serving plates and serve.

THREE PEPPER ROASTED SHRIMP

Just about everyone likes shrimp. If your guests crave spicy foods, they'll enjoy this fresh, tasty dish. For a stunning presentation, serve it over steamed rice accompanied by a fresh green salad. Habanero chiles are extremely hot. Substitute a milder variety if desired, such as a serrano or jalapeño, or use ¼ to ½ of the habanero.

1 tbs. fresh lemon juice
1 tsp. fresh lime juice
1 tbs. grated ginger root
1 tbs. dry white wine
1 tsp. dried coriander leaves
1 tsp. grated fresh lemon peel (zest)
¼ tsp. freshly ground pepper

1 jalapeño pepper, seeded, sliced
salt to taste
1 medium red bell pepper, seeded, diced
1 habanero pepper, seeded, chopped
1 lb. large shrimp, peeled, deveined
hot cooked white rice

Combine all ingredients, except shrimp and rice, in a large bowl and mix well. Add shrimp and stir until completely coated. Cover bowl and marinate shrimp for 1 hour in the refrigerator.

Heat oven to 400°. Place shrimp mixture in a medium roasting pan and roast for 5 minutes. Stir mixture and roast for about 5 minutes, until shrimp are just cooked through. Serve immediately over individual portions of rice.

ROASTED CLAMS AND MUSSELS

Servings: 4

Purchase fresh-smelling clams and mussels with closed shells and no visible cracks from a reputable seafood merchant. After roasting, discard shellfish that did not open. It is said that to avoid contamination, eat shellfish only in those months of the year that contain the letter "R." Serve over cooked fresh pasta, steamed brown rice or thick slices of country bread.

1 lb. clams in shells (littlenecks or soft shell)
1 lb. mussels in shells
3 cloves garlic, minced or pressed
1/4 cup fresh lemon juice
2 tbs. dry white wine

1/4 cup finely chopped fresh parsley
1/2 tsp. freshly ground pepper
salt to taste
1 tsp. red pepper flakes
2 tbs. butter, cut into small pieces

Heat oven to 500°. Scrub clams and mussels thoroughly with a stiff brush under cold running water and remove beards from mussels. Place clams and mussels in a large roasting pan. In a small bowl, combine garlic, lemon juice, wine, parsley, ground pepper, salt and pepper flakes and mix well. Pour mixture over clams and mussels and toss once or twice to coat. Scatter butter among clams and mussels. Roast for 10 to 12 minutes, turning once or twice, or until shells pop open. Discard any unopened clams or mussels. Serve immediately with roasting liquid as sauce.

ROASTED SCALLOPS AU GRATIN

Servings: 4

This is our favorite recipe for scallops. It's quick and easy to prepare with a simple, exquisite flavor. The crusty roasted breadcrumb topping is equally delicious over other seafood casseroles of shrimp or mild, delicate fish including cod, flounder, scrod, haddock, halibut, grouper, snapper and sole.

3 tbs. breadcrumbs
1 tbs. butter, melted
1 clove garlic, minced or pressed
2 lb. sea scallops
1 tbs. fresh lemon juice

$\frac{1}{4}$ tsp. dried basil
$\frac{1}{4}$ tsp. dried oregano
$\frac{1}{8}$ tsp. freshly ground pepper
salt to taste
$\frac{1}{8}$ tsp. paprika

Heat oven to 450°. Lightly coat a medium roasting pan or 4 small ovenproof casserole dishes with nonstick cooking spray. In a small bowl, combine breadcrumbs, butter and garlic; mix thoroughly and set aside. Rinse scallops and pat dry. Place scallops in roasting pan and drizzle with lemon juice. Top with a layer of breadcrumb mixture and sprinkle with basil, oregano, pepper, salt and paprika. Roast for 12 to 15 minutes, until scallops turn opaque.

ROTISSERIE ROASTING

ABOUT ROTISSERIE ROASTING

Roasting foods on a slow turning, motorized rotisserie is a thrilling, visually appealing way to prepare foods. Foods turn constantly over an evenly distributed heat source, producing wonderful textures and flavors. Portable rotisseries are readily available in department stores, specialty housewares shops, home center hardware stores and at most wholesale clubs. Anything that can be attached to a spit can be roasted on a rotisserie.

With portable electric rotisseries, the heating element is set below a grill rack and a drip pan sits below the heating element. A motorized spit extends above the heating element and can be set at various heights. Foods are secured to the spit with holding forks that rotate over the heat source. Because food is constantly turning, the dripping liquids produce a self-basting action and food roasts evenly. Incredibly, the design of portable ovens allows for nearly complete smokeless and splatter-free roasting and there's no carbon build-up. Rotisseries take only a few minutes to assemble and they store very easily. They are lightweight and clean easily since most parts are dishwasher safe.

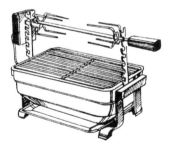

GUIDELINES FOR OPERATING A PORTABLE ROTISSERIE

- Position the food as close to the heating element as possible, but do not let the food make contact with the heating element as it turns.

- Truss or fasten the legs and wings of poultry securely (see page 3).

- Be sure the food is balanced on the spit so that it roasts evenly and does not interfere with the motorized operation.

- Rotisseries come in various sizes. Be sure the food does not extend beyond the length of the heating element.

- When roasting 2 or more items on a spit, such as Cornish hens, leave 1 to 2 inches of space between items for proper heat circulation.

- Heating elements may vary with different models, so follow the manufacturer's suggestions for roasting times. For the most accurate indication of doneness, use a meat thermometer.

- Shut off the motor and heating element and unplug the rotisserie unit before taking roasted foods off the spit.

You can also prepare these recipes on an outdoor charcoal, gas or electric grill equipped with a mechanically turned rotisserie, but be sure to follow the manufacturer's instructions.

ROTISSERIE-ROASTED EGGPLANT DIP

Yield: 2 cups

Fresh farmstand eggplants often taste best. When purchasing eggplant the skin should feel firm, but not too hard. Serve this dip with chips or crackers, or as a spread for sandwiches.

1 large eggplant
$\frac{1}{2}$ tsp. plus 1 tbs. olive oil
1 tbs. fresh lemon juice
2 tbs. chopped scallions
$\frac{1}{8}$ tsp. ground cumin

$\frac{1}{8}$ tsp. dried marjoram
1 clove garlic, minced or pressed
salt and pepper to taste
paprika for garnish
chopped fresh parsley for garnish

Prick eggplant with a fork in several places and rub evenly with $\frac{1}{2}$ tsp. olive oil. Secure and balance eggplant on the spit. Set spit as close to heating element as possible so that eggplant does not touch as it turns. Turn on motor and heating element and roast eggplant for 40 to 45 minutes until skin is blackened. Turn off motor and heating element, remove eggplant and cool. Peel charred skin from eggplant and discard. Cut eggplant into small pieces. Combine eggplant pieces, 1 tbs. olive oil, lemon juice, scallions, cumin, marjoram, garlic, salt and pepper in a food processor workbowl or blender container and process until smooth. Transfer to a serving bowl and sprinkle with paprika and parsley. Serve chilled.

SPIT-ROASTED FIGS AND PROSCIUTTO

Here's a new way to excite your taste buds. This dish tastes every bit as good as it sounds. It's completely satisfying with an elegant and out-of-the-ordinary presentation.

4 thin slices prosciutto
8 fresh figs, trimmed
apricot preserves
1 lb. Gorgonzola cheese, cut into bite-sized pieces
fresh green and red grapes

Cut prosciutto in half lengthwise, wrap around figs and secure each wrapped fig to a prong on the holding forks of the spit. Side should be balanced. Set spit as close to the heating element as possible so that figs do not touch as they turn. Turn on motor and heating element and roast figs for 10 to 12 minutes, brushing with apricot preserves several times during roasting. Turn off motor and heating element and remove figs. Cool. Place prosciutto-wrapped figs on a serving platter with cheese and fresh grapes.

ROTISSERIE-ROASTED ZUCCHINI

Servings: 2

*This is one of our favorite methods for preparing zucchini or any freshly picked summer squash. For a real treat, substitute **Roasted Garlic Oil**, page 16, for olive oil, and, at only 20 calories per tablespoon, the freshly grated Parmesan cheese packs in a lot of flavor.*

2 medium zucchini
olive oil for basting
2 tbs. freshly grated Parmesan or Romano cheese

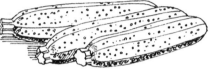

Trim ends from zucchini and cut in half lengthwise. Secure and balance zucchini on the spit. Each side should be well balanced. Set spit as close to the heating element as possible so that zucchini does not touch as it turns. Turn on motor and heating element and roast zucchini for 20 to 25 minutes until tender, brushing occasionally with olive oil. Turn off motor and heating element and remove zucchini. Serve warm with grated cheese.

SPIT-ROASTED CORNISH GAME HENS WITH ORANGE-APRICOT GLAZE

Servings: 2

This makes a wonderfully succulent and economical meal with no added butter or oil. Serve hens over a bed of your favorite rice along with a tossed green salad.

5 tbs. apricot preserves
3 tbs. orange juice
2 rock Cornish game hens, about 20 oz. each

salt and pepper to taste
1 medium orange, quartered
parsley sprigs for garnish, optional

In a small bowl, combine apricot preserves and orange juice. Remove giblets from hens and discard. Rinse hens and pat dry. Sprinkle hen cavities with salt and pepper. Place 2 orange quarters into cavity of each hen. Position wings behind hen and truss hens with kitchen string (see page 3). Secure and balance hens on the spit, leaving a 2-inch space between hens. Set spit as close to the heating element as possible so that hens do not touch as they turn. Turn on motor and heating element and roast for 1¼ to 1½ hours, until a thermometer inserted in the breast reads 175°, or until juices run clear when thickest part of breast is pierced with a knife. Baste occasionally with orange-apricot sauce. Turn off motor and heating element, remove hens and place on warm individual serving plates. Garnish with sprigs of parsley if desired.

ROTISSERIE-ROASTED LEMON-HERB CHICKEN WITH PAN GRAVY

Servings: 4-6

To ensure a moist and flavorful chicken, let it sit for 10 minutes after it's roasted so the juices can redistribute throughout the bird.

2 lemons, halved
1 roasting chicken, about 6-6½ lb.
¼ tsp. salt
¼ tsp. freshly ground pepper
2 cloves garlic, minced
½ tsp. dried basil
¼ tsp. dried oregano
1 cup low-sodium chicken stock
2 tbs. flour

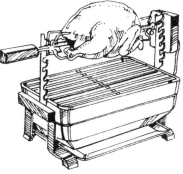

Squeeze juice from lemon halves into a small bowl and set aside. Remove giblets and neck from chicken and discard. Rinse chicken, pat dry and sprinkle chicken cavity with ⅛ tsp. of the salt and ⅛ tsp. of the pepper. Place lemon halves and garlic into cavity and close cavity securely with skewers and kitchen string. Truss chicken securely (see page 3). Brush chicken with lemon juice and sprinkle with basil, oregano and remaining salt and pepper.

Secure and balance chicken on rotisserie spit. Set spit as close to the heating element as possible so that chicken does not touch as it turns. Turn on motor and heating element and roast for 1¾ to 2¼ hours, until a thermometer inserted in the breast reads 170°, or until juices run clear when thickest part of breast is pierced with a knife. Baste with lemon juice every 15 to 20 minutes. Turn off motor and heating element, remove chicken and let sit for 10 minutes before carving into serving pieces.

Pour pan drippings into a fat separator or bowl; remove fat and discard. Pour juices into a small saucepan. Mix cold stock with flour, add to saucepan and whisk continuously over medium-high heat. Bring to a quick boil and reduce heat to medium. Continue whisking until gravy thickens. Serve over chicken pieces.

SPIT-ROASTED DUCK WITH PLUM SAUCE

Servings: 2-3

If plums are out of season, you can purchase jars of plum sauce at most supermarkets, Asian grocery stores and specialty food shops. For a variation, serve applesauce or cranberry sauce in place of the plum sauce.

4 purple plums, pitted, minced
2 cloves garlic, minced or pressed
¼ cup orange marmalade
¼ cup low-sodium soy sauce

¼ cup orange juice
2 tbs. Dijon mustard
1 tbs. rice vinegar
1 duck, about 4-5 lb.

Combine all ingredients, except duck, in a saucepan over low heat. Bring to a slow boil, stirring frequently, and cook for 8 to 10 minutes. Remove from heat and transfer to a serving bowl. Serve warm, or chill in the refrigerator for 2 to 3 hours before serving.

Remove giblets, neck and excess fat from duck cavity. Rinse duck and pat dry. Prick duck skin in several places with the tines of a fork. Secure wings behind duck and tie legs together. Secure and balance duck on the spit. Set spit as close to the heating element as possible so that duck doesn't touch as it turns. Turn on motor and heating element and roast duck for 1½ to 2 hours, until a thermometer inserted in the breast reads 175°, or until juices run clear when thickest part of breast is pierced with a knife. Turn off motor and heating element. Remove duck from rotisserie and let sit for 10 to 15 minutes before carving. Spoon plum sauce over duck pieces.

SPIT-ROASTED SPARERIBS

Servings: 3-4

These beautifully flavored and brilliantly glazed spareribs are great for a social setting — just be sure to serve them with lots of napkins. The aroma is fabulous.

1 tbs. olive or canola oil
1 tbs. minced shallots
1/4 cup honey
1/4 cup dry sherry
1 tsp. freshly grated ginger root
1 tbs. brown sugar, packed
1/2 tsp. dry mustard
1/8 tsp. freshly ground pepper
2 racks pork spareribs, 6-8 ribs each

In a small skillet, heat oil over medium heat. Add shallots and sauté for 2 to 3 minutes, until soft. Combine all ingredients, except ribs, in a small bowl and mix well. Secure and balance spareribs on the spit. Set spit as close to the heating element as possible so that ribs do not touch as they turn. Turn on motor and heating element. Roast ribs for 1 to 1 1/2 hours, until desired doneness, brushing frequently with sauce. Turn off motor and heating element and remove ribs. Separate ribs and serve warm.

ROTISSERIE-ROASTED HAM
WITH FRESH PEACH AND APPLE CHUTNEY

This is ideal for a Sunday afternoon meal. If you have any ham leftover, it's a great addition to risotto or an omelet. The fresh fruit chutney adds flair to any type of pork.

4½-5 lb. boneless, fully cooked smoked ham
2 large peaches, peeled, chopped
1 large Granny Smith apple, peeled, chopped
⅓ cup golden raisins
¼ cup chopped shallots
1 jalapeño pepper, seeded, minced
3 tbs. fresh orange juice
2 tbs. pure maple syrup
½ tsp. cinnamon

Trim excess fat and rind from ham. Lightly score the outside of ham in a diamond pattern. Secure and balance ham on the spit. Set spit as close as possible to the heating element so that ham does not touch as it turns. Turn on motor and heating element and roast ham for about 2 hours, until a thermometer inserted in the center reads 140°.

While ham is roasting, combine peaches, apple, raisins, shallots, jalapeño, orange juice, maple syrup and cinnamon in a medium saucepan. Bring to a boil, reduce heat to low and simmer, partially covered, for 35 to 40 minutes until tender, but not mushy. Cool and refrigerate, or set aside until ready to serve.

Turn off rotisserie motor and heating element. Remove ham and let sit, covered, for 10 minutes before slicing. If desired, heat chutney over low heat until bubbling and serve over sliced ham.

ROTISSERIE-ROASTED PORK
WITH PEANUT SAUCE

Hoisin sauce is a thick and spicy condiment made from soy beans, chili paste, vinegar and garlic. It's a common ingredient in many Asian recipes. Hoisin sauce can be found in most supermarkets, Asian markets and specialty food shops.

3 tbs. creamy peanut butter
2 tbs. water
1 tbs. fresh lemon juice
1½ tbs. low-sodium soy sauce
¼ cup hoisin sauce
1 tbs. honey
½ tsp. sesame oil
2 cloves garlic, minced or pressed
1 tsp. grated ginger root
1 boneless pork loin roast, about 2-3 lb., tied securely

In a small bowl, whisk together all ingredients, except pork. Divide peanut sauce into 2 equal portions and refrigerate 1 portion until needed. Secure and balance pork on the spit. Set spit as close to the heating element as possible so that pork does not touch as it turns. Turn on motor and heating element and roast pork for about 1½ hours, until a thermometer inserted in the center reads 160°. Baste often with unrefrigerated peanut sauce. Turn off motor and heating element. Remove pork and let sit, covered, for 10 minutes before slicing. Bring refrigerated peanut sauce to room temperature and serve with sliced pork.

SPIT-ROASTED VEAL WITH SAUTÉED APPLES

Servings: 3-5

The olive oil-herb mixture forms a delicate glaze as the veal slowly roasts on the rotisserie.

2 tbs. olive oil
¼ tsp. dried thyme
¼ tsp. dried sage
½ tsp. dried marjoram
⅛ tsp. freshly ground pepper
salt to taste
1 rolled shoulder veal roast, about 3-5 lb., tied securely
3 cups *Roasted Apple Sauté*, page 19

In a small bowl, combine olive oil, thyme, sage, marjoram, pepper and salt. Secure and balance veal securely on the spit. Set spit as close to the heating element as possible so that veal does not touch as it turns. Turn on motor and heating element and roast veal for 2¼ hours or until a thermometer inserted in the center reads 170°. Baste often with olive oil herb mixture. Turn off motor and heating element, remove veal and let sit, covered, for 10 minutes before slicing. Slice veal and serve with warm *Roasted Apple Sauté*.

ROASTED DESSERTS

ROASTED PEACHES WITH COCONUT

Servings: 4

This recipe takes an ordinary peach and turns it into an extraordinary dessert. This is sure to bring you many compliments. To peel fresh peaches, place them in a pot of boiling water for 10 seconds and transfer them immediately to a bowl of ice cold water. The skins will rub off effortlessly.

4 large peaches, peeled, cut into 6 wedges
½ cup butter, melted
3 tbs. brown sugar, packed
½ tsp. ground ginger
2 tbs. shredded coconut
vanilla ice cream, optional

Heat oven to 375°. Place peach wedges in a medium roasting pan. In a small bowl, combine melted butter, brown sugar and ginger and drizzle over peaches. Roast peaches for 20 minutes. Heat broiler. Sprinkle peaches with coconut and place under broiler for 2 to 3 minutes, until coconut is golden brown. Serve warm or chilled over individual portions of ice cream if desired.

MAPLE-GLAZED ROASTED APRICOTS

Servings: 3-4

If fresh apricots are not in season, you can substitute drained canned apricots. Serve them as a dessert with ice cream, frozen yogurt or whipped cream. They're also scrumptious as a side dish for pork, fish or poultry.

8 fresh apricots, halved
2 tbs. butter, cut into small pieces
1/4 cup pure maple syrup

Heat oven to 375°. Lightly coat a small roasting pan with nonstick cooking spray. Place apricots in roasting pan skin-side down, dot with butter and drizzle with maple syrup. Roast for 6 to 7 minutes, until tender. Heat broiler. Place apricots under broiler for 2 to 3 minutes until a crust forms.

ROASTED SPICED PEARS

Servings: 4

This collection of spices adds a beautiful flavor and aroma without overpowering the distinctive taste of the roasted pears.

4 medium-sized ripe pears
2 oranges
$\frac{1}{2}$ tsp. cinnamon
$\frac{1}{8}$ tsp. ground cloves

dash ground cardamom, optional
$\frac{1}{3}$ cup brown sugar, packed
frozen yogurt or ice cream, optional

Heat oven to 400°. Peel pears and slice in half lengthwise. Use a spoon to remove cores. Lay pear halves snugly in a small ovenproof dish, taking care not to overlap. Squeeze juice from oranges into a small bowl and discard seeds. Add cinnamon, cloves, cardamom, if using, and brown sugar to orange juice and mix well. Pour mixture over pears. Roast for 35 to 40 minutes, basting pears occasionally with pan juices and turning pears over after the first 15 minutes of roasting. Remove from oven and serve on individual dessert plates. Serve over individual portions of ice cream or frozen yogurt if desired.

ROASTED STUFFED APPLES

Servings: 4

This is an ideal dessert to prepare during the chilly fall months when the best-tasting apples are in the height of their season. Choose from the large variety of cooking apples including Baldwin, Cortland, Golden Delicious, Granny Smith, Gravenstein, Ida Red, Jonathan, Macoun and Northern Spy.

2-3 tbs. sugar
2 tbs. golden raisins
1 tbs. finely chopped walnuts
1 tbs. finely chopped pecans
1 tbs. finely chopped almonds
1 tsp. cinnamon
1/2 tsp. ground cardamom

1/4 tsp. ground cloves
1/4 cup butter, melted
1 tbs. brown sugar, packed
2 tbs. canola oil
4 medium apples, peeled, halved
   horizontally, cores removed
French vanilla ice cream, optional

Heat oven to 375°. In a small bowl, combine sugar, raisins, nuts, cinnamon, cardamom and cloves. In another small bowl, combine melted butter and brown sugar. Brush a medium roasting pan with canola oil. Place apple halves in pan, cored-side up. Place equal amounts of nut mixture in each apple cavity and drizzle with butter and brown sugar mixture. Roast apples for about 20 minutes, until tender. Heat broiler. Place apples under broiler for 2 to 3 minutes, until lightly browned. Serve alone or with scoops of French vanilla ice cream.

ROASTED FIGS

Servings: 3-4

While working on this book, we had the good fortune of treating ourselves to an abundance of fresh figs from Dave's father's orchard of fig trees. This allowed us to happily test and retest this delicious and richly flavored dessert. If you're a backyard gardener, consider planting a few fig trees. They're easy to maintain and can provide you with a lifetime supply of enjoyment.

6 fresh figs
½ cup apple juice
¼ tsp. cinnamon
3 tbs. chopped walnuts
frozen yogurt, optional

Heat oven to 425°. Trim ends from figs and cut in half lengthwise. Place figs cut-side down in a small ceramic baking dish. Pour apple juice over figs, sprinkle with cinnamon and roast for 5 to 6 minutes. Remove from oven, sprinkle with chopped walnuts and serve warm. Or, spoon warm figs over individual dishes of frozen yogurt and sprinkle with chopped walnuts.

ROASTED BANANAS ROYALE

You can prepare this elegant, mouth-watering tropical dessert any time of the year. For best results, use firm bananas that are just a bit underripe.

4 bananas
juice from 1 lemon
2 tbs. butter, melted
1/3 cup brown sugar, packed
1/3 tsp. cinnamon

1/8 tsp. nutmeg
1/3 cup coarsely chopped walnuts
confectioners' sugar for garnish,
  optional

Heat oven to 375°. Peel and slice each banana in half lengthwise. Place bananas cut-side up in a lightly greased roasting pan. Roast for 6 minutes and remove from oven.

In a small bowl, combine lemon juice, butter, brown sugar, cinnamon and nutmeg and mix well. Drizzle mixture over bananas and sprinkle with chopped walnuts. Return pan to oven and roast for 3 minutes. Remove from oven and place bananas on individual serving plates. Drizzle bananas with pan juices and, if desired, garnish with confectioners' sugar.

ROASTED FRESH PINEAPPLE
WITH CILANTRO

Servings: 4-6

This makes a delightful alternative when you're searching for something completely different for dessert. You'll find parchment paper in housewares shops and in some department stores.

1 large pineapple
3 tbs. unsweetened pineapple juice
1 tbs. honey
½ tsp. ground ginger
⅛ tsp. ground cloves
2 tbs. chopped fresh cilantro
vanilla ice cream, optional

Heat oven to 400°. Peel, core and cut pineapple into 10 to 12 slices. In a small bowl, whisk together pineapple juice, honey, ginger, cloves and cilantro. Place pineapple slices on a parchment-lined rimmed baking sheet and drizzle with cilantro mixture. Roast for 12 to 13 minutes. Remove from oven and serve with scoops of vanilla ice cream for dessert, or alone as an appetizer.

ROASTED GRAPEFRUIT

Servings: 2-4

You can serve this exceptionally tasty fruit preparation alone on small serving plates, or over crumbled amaretto cookies or graham crackers.

2 pink grapefruits
2 tbs. maple syrup
2 tbs. brown sugar, packed
½ tsp. cinnamon

Heat oven to 400°. Peel grapefruits and separate into sections. Remove and discard seeds and pith. Place grapefruit sections in 2 small ovenproof casseroles, taking care not to overlap. Drizzle grapefruit sections with maple syrup and sprinkle with brown sugar and cinnamon. Roast for 15 minutes. Serve warm.

ROASTED STRAWBERRIES

Serve these on small serving plates or over frozen yogurt, ice cream, French toast, waffles, pancakes, shortcakes or angel food cake topped with whipped cream.

½ tbs. water
24 fresh strawberries
1 tsp. honey
1 tbs. butter, melted
½ tbs. granulated sugar
½ tbs. brown sugar, packed
⅛ tsp. cinnamon

Heat oven to 375°. Pour water into a small roasting pan. Hull strawberries and place in a single layer in pan, stem-side down. Drizzle strawberries with honey, melted butter, sugars and cinnamon. Roast for 7 minutes. Remove strawberries from pan and serve immediately.

ROASTED CHESTNUT BISCOTTI

This is one of our favorite treats. Add a steaming cup of cafe latté or cappuccino, and you've got the perfect recipe for a memorable dessert. You can store these in the freezer for up to 6 months. They will thaw within 20 minutes at room temperature.

1¼ cups all-purpose flour
1 tsp. baking powder
pinch salt
2 tbs. butter, softened
½ cup sugar

1 egg
1½ tsp. pure vanilla extract
½ cup finely chopped roasted
  chestnuts (see page 10)

Heat oven to 350°. Sift flour, baking powder and salt together; set aside. With an electric mixer, cream butter and sugar. Add egg and mix well. Add vanilla and mix until blended. Add flour mixture and beat until well mixed. Mix in chopped roasted chestnuts. Form dough into a 14-x-3-inch loaf, place on a parchment-lined baking sheet and bake for 30 minutes. Remove from oven and cool for 5 to 10 minutes on a wire rack. Cut loaf into ½-inch slices, place on baking sheet and bake for 5 minutes. Turn slices over and bake for 5 minutes. Place biscotti on a wire rack to cool. Store in an airtight container.

ROASTED CHESTNUT AND CHOCOLATE MOUNDS

Yield: about 15

This rich-tasting chocolate dessert is actually relatively low in fat. If you're making a double or triple batch, the same sheet of parchment paper can be used several times.

¼ cup low-fat sweetened condensed milk
2 oz. unsweetened baking chocolate, chopped
⅓ cup semisweet chocolate chips
2 egg whites
1 tbs. nonfat (skim) milk

½ tsp. pure vanilla extract
½ cup all-purpose flour
¾ tsp. baking powder
⅛ tsp. salt, optional
½ cup finely chopped roasted chestnuts (see page 10)

Heat oven to 350°. In a medium saucepan or the top of a double boiler, combine sweetened condensed milk, unsweetened chocolate and chocolate chips. Heat over low heat or simmering water until chocolate is melted. Remove from heat. Add egg whites, skim milk and vanilla and mix well. Mix in flour, baking powder and salt, if using, and stir in chopped chestnuts. Drop rounded teaspoons of dough on a parchment-lined baking sheet. Bake for 8 minutes. Cool cookies on a wire rack.

INDEX

SERVE CREATIVE, EASY, NUTRITIOUS MEALS WITH nitty gritty® COOKBOOKS

Edible Pockets for Every Meal
Cooking With Chile Peppers
Oven and Rotisserie Roasting
Risottos, Paellas and Other Rice
  Specialties
Entrées From Your Bread Machine
Muffins, Nut Breads and More
Healthy Snacks for Kids
100 Dynamite Desserts
Recipes for Yogurt Cheese
Sautés
Cooking in Porcelain
Appetizers
Casseroles
The Best Bagels are made at home*
  (*perfect for your bread machine)
The Toaster Oven Cookbook
Skewer Cooking on the Grill
Creative Mexican Cooking
Extra-Special Crockery Pot Recipes
Slow Cooking
Cooking in Clay
Marinades
Deep Fried Indulgences

Cooking with Parchment Paper
The Garlic Cookbook
From Your Ice Cream Maker
Cappuccino/Espresso: The Book of
  Beverages
The Best Pizza is made at home*
  (*perfect for your bread machine)
The Well Dressed Potato
Convection Oven Cookery
The Steamer Cookbook
The Pasta Machine Cookbook
The Versatile Rice Cooker
The Dehydrator Cookbook
The Bread Machine Cookbook
The Bread Machine Cookbook II
The Bread Machine Cookbook III
The Bread Machine Cookbook IV:
  Whole Grains and Natural Sugars
The Bread Machine Cookbook V:
  Favorite Recipes from 100 Kitchens
The Bread Machine Cookbook VI:
  *Hand-Shaped Breads from the
  Dough Cycle*

Worldwide Sourdoughs From Your
  Bread Machine
Recipes for the Pressure Cooker
The New Blender Book
The Sandwich Maker Cookbook
Waffles
Indoor Grilling
The Coffee Book
The Juicer Books I and II
Bread Baking (traditional)
No Salt, No Sugar, No Fat Cookbook
Cooking for 1 or 2
Quick and Easy Pasta Recipes
The 9x13 Pan Cookbook
Recipes for the Loaf Pan
Low Fat American Favorites
Now That's Italian!
Healthy Cooking on the Run
The Wok
Favorite Seafood Recipes
New International Fondue Cookbook
Favorite Cookie Recipes
Flatbreads From Around the World

For a free catalog, write or call:
Bristol Publishing Enterprises, Inc.
P.O. Box 1737, San Leandro, CA 94577
(800) 346-4889; in California, (510) 895-4461